MARKETING WITH SPEECHES AND SEMINARS

EVERYONE IS TALKING ABOUT...

MARKETING WITH SPEECHES AND SEMINARS

"In an easy-to-read style, Miriam Otte shows how to turn your expertise into marketing power for your business, and generate a continuous stream of customers. Here's all you need to know to talk your way to business success. Even the terminally shy will find that marketing has never been easier — or more fun!"

– Terri Lonier, small business expert
and author of *Working Solo*

"Miriam Otte has written an invaluable guide for any small business owner who hopes to market their business through speeches and seminars ... Miriam reaches a hand out and offers direction, helpful advice, and best of all, very specific details on how to get the job done well. I would recommend this book to any small business owner."

– Azriela Jaffe, author of *Honey, I Want to Start My Own Business: A Planning Guide for Couples*

"*Marketing with Speeches and Seminars* is a comprehensive, clearly written, easy-to-follow manual for anyone who wants to sell their products/services through this medium. Everything you need to know is in the book. I plan to keep my copy on a nearby bookshelf for ready reference."

– Michael LeBoeuf, Ph.D.,
author of *The Perfect Business*

MARKETING WITH SPEECHES AND SEMINARS

Your Key to More Clients and Referrals

Miriam Otte, MSW, CPA

PUSTAK MAHAL®
Delhi • Bangalore • Mumbai • Patna • Hyderabad • London

Copyright © in India by
Pustak Mahal®, Delhi
J-3/16 , Daryaganj, New Delhi-110002
☎ 23276539, 23272783, 23272784 • *Fax:* 011-23260518
E-mail: info@pustakmahal.com • *Website:* www.pustakmahal.com

London Office
5, Roddell Court, Bath Road, Slough SL3 OQJ, England
E-mail: pustakmahaluk@pustakmahal.com

Sales Centre
10-B, Netaji Subhash Marg, Daryaganj, New Delhi-110002
☎ 23268292, 23268293, 23279900 • *Fax:* 011-23280567
E-mail: rapidexdelhi@indiatimes.com

Branch Offices
Bangalore: ☎ 22234025
E-mail: pmblr@sancharnet.in • pustak@sancharnet.in
Mumbai: ☎ 22010941
E-mail: rapidex@bom5.vsnl.net.in
Patna: ☎ 3294193 • *Telefax:* 0612-2302719
E-mail: rapidexptn@rediffmail.com
Hyderabad: *Telefax:* 040-24737290
E-mail: pustakmahalhyd@yahoo.co.in

Published in India by arrangement with
ZEST PRESS
U.S.A.

ISBN 978-81-223-0424-4

Printed at : S.K. Enterprises, Delhi

DEDICATION

*To my own personal cheerleader:
my husband, Don Johnson.*

ACKNOWLEDGMENTS

Grateful acknowledgment is made to the women of Alderlynn Toastmistress Club: Joan Brown, Elaine Klein, Rosa Ranson, Lois Warren, Kitty Willis and especially Verna Rauscher, who helped an extremely nervous me become a professional speaker.

CONTENTS

INTRODUCTION

This is the book I always wanted to refer to.

Lots of experts tell us that public speaking is an excellent way to get clients and referrals. But there are two major things they don't tell you:

1. The step-by-step procedures for giving speeches and seminars;
2. Practical techniques for overcoming the fear of public speaking.

This book does both.

Oh sure, there are tons of books on speaking, but most of them assume you want to become a professional speaker or that you need to make a presentation to your boss. This book will teach you how to use speaking as a marketing tool.

In this day and age, finding clients and cultivating referrals can be tough. The competition is fierce. And many of your prospects have been bombarded with sales material. They may desperately need your services but are hesitant to trust someone they do not know. Speaking is the perfect venue for establishing a credible relationship with these folks. They get to audition you. Try before they buy. See if you are the type of person they would like to do business with.

And you have the opportunity to pitch to a room full of qualified prospects. That sure beats making cold calls! Or a measly 2% response on a direct mail campaign!

It all sounds wonderful and it is. Or can be if it wasn't for this gnawing reality that just the thought of presenting a speech or seminar can be terrifying. I know. Believe me, I know. Let's be clear from the beginning that I am not a "natural-born" speaker. I've given thousands of presentations and I still get nervous. Really nervous.

I know about terror. When I first realized that my fear of public speaking was getting in the way of my success, I could barely stand up and say my name in front of others. I was absolutely sure that my trembling knees would not support me. Friendly folks in my audiences would suggest that I sip some water to calm down, and it would end up all over me because I was shaking so badly. (Funny now, mortifying then!)

That's why this book is chock full of suggestions on what to do to manage your fear and get your message across. I'll share what has worked for me. I assure you that you do not need to be a slick presenter in order to attain your marketing goals. In fact, you may come to realize that just being yourself—even a nervous self—may make you more attractive to your prospects. Believe me, they will relate. And they'll appreciate your good intentions.

No longer do you need to let your fear of public speaking get in the way of your success. You will experience a special thrill in overcoming an obstacle that has stifled you from fully developing in your profession.

HERE'S WHAT'S IN STORE FOR YOU

In Chapter 1 we'll zoom right into where you can find your target folks in an audience that needs a presenter—that's you. Plus you'll get lots of ideas on how you can create your own speaking opportunities.

Chapter 2 will be invaluable to you in developing the topics you wish to speak on. It will show you how to focus on what you like to talk about and the needs of your prospects. You'll become crystal-clear as to why people should come and hear your talk. This material will make it easier for you to book your speaking gigs. You'll learn how to come up with a great title and a compelling description of your talk.

Chapter 3 gives you lots of tips on how to create a successful presentation that your audience will perceive as being valuable. It includes seven ways to add interest. And scads of other gems to include in your talk.

If you decide to present speeches, Chapter 4 will be the one you will refer to again and again. It gives you a choice of two easy-to-follow formulas for developing your speeches.

If you decide to give seminars, Chapter 5 is where you will go to learn a simple formula for creating a successful seminar.

Chapter 6 gives you the steps to successfully book your presentations. Whether you decide to pitch your speech to a meeting planner or sponsor your own seminar, you'll have the techniques for accomplishing your goals with the least hassle and in the shortest amount of time.

In order for your efforts to pay off you'll need lots of great prospects in your audience. Chapter 7 gives practical suggestions on how to market your talk. It shows you the nine items that should be in your marketing tool kit. Plus it gives you 20 ways to market yourself and your presentations.

Pitching your products and services from the platform can be challenging. Chapter 8 teaches you seven of the best ways to make it work for you.

The next five chapters will provide you with lots of advice on how to handle the details that contribute to giving a successful speech or seminar. In Chapter 9 you'll learn how to maximize your preparation time. It covers room set-up, handouts, notes, your introduction and what to do at your practice sessions. Chapter 10 suggests that you always use some sort of visual aid to make your message more effective. You'll find out how to use the most common visual-aid equipment and the advantages and disadvantages of each kind. In Chapter 11 you're provided with step-by-step guidelines for handling the infinite details on the day of your presentation. This chapter also includes a valuable section on how to effectively use any microphone you may encounter. Chapter 12 is full of delivery techniques that will help even the driest topic come alive. And Chapter 13 will give you proven methods to becoming a dynamite presenter and getting any nervousness under control.

Chapter 14 takes you through the steps you'll take to turn the folks in your audience into clients and referral sources.

Chapter 15 is a bonus chapter for you, just in case you get hooked on public speaking and decide to make it a lucrative profit center. You'll learn five steps to getting paid for your presentations and ten ways to make money speaking.

This book also includes a large appendix that is going to greatly reduce the time and effort you'll need before you start speaking. Besides the usual list of reference books and resource information, there are lots of examples of the type of material you'll need to develop in order to market your talks. Plus, there are four invaluable checklists you'll use before, the day of, and just after your presentations. Use them over and over again, so that you will be more successful.

HOW TO GET YOUR MONEY'S WORTH FROM THIS BOOK

As I said, this is the book I always wanted for reference when I was building my small business consulting firm. I hope you will find it so useful that you return to it time and time again.

Read it with a highlighter or pen in hand—unless it's a library copy! Then purchase one for your very own by going to your local bookstore or completing the order form in the back of this book.

SPEAKING AS A MARKETING TOOL

This book is densely packed with information. It will help you dramatically increase your clientele and the number of referrals you get.

When you use speaking as a marketing tool, you will discover another amazing phenomenon. Public speaking establishes you as an expert. You will start to attract new clients from people who have never heard you speak but want to work with you anyway. You will get referrals from colleagues and other professionals in complementary fields who associate you and your expertise with the subject you speak about.

You entered your profession because you are passionate about the work. Or, at least, I hope so. You know that your work can make a significant difference in people's lives. Giving speeches and seminars helps you to get your message across to the people who really need it. It lets people see that you are a person they can trust, and makes them feel that they can't wait to start to work with you.

I wish you outrageous success.

1

FINDING AUDIENCES FULL OF PROSPECTIVE CLIENTS AND REFERRAL SOURCES

Once you know who your target prospects are, it's easy to locate them in audiences or to create your own speaking opportunities.

THE VALUE OF NICHING

Niching is a key concept that applies not only to business but also to speaking. Take a look at what others in your field are speaking about and to whom they are speaking. You'll probably find that the successful ones focus on a particular niche audience or around a particular subject. The speakers are perceived as the experts in that specific niche. They are often the ones asked by the group to speak.

Is there a particular subject or audience you can specialize in? Let's say you are a Certified Financial Planner. Rather than speaking to everyone and anyone on general topics of financial planning, you decide to specialize. Your niche is women or widows. That will make your presentation much more focused and single you out from your competition.

Or let's say you are a therapist. You decide to specialize in the effect of divorce on children. Now you have a hot topic that will be eagerly picked up by most any group you propose to address.

Don't think that because you have decided to niche you will be stuck there forever—although you might find it enjoyable and very lucrative. Next year you can add another niche and start the whole speaking process again.

DEFINE YOUR IDEAL CLIENTS

Let's take a look now at your "ideal clients." You may have already defined this group as part of your business planning process, but it's important to take another look as we focus on increasing your clientele and referrals through speaking.

Whether your target clients are individuals, people in certain professions or decision-makers in particular companies, it is imperative that you know a lot about them. Describe them—age, sex, income level, education, work experience, where they live, hobbies, etc. Of course, the more clear your idea of whom you are targeting, the easier it becomes to find them.

WHAT AUDIENCES ARE YOUR PROSPECTS IN?

Now here's the most valuable part of your client profile: What groups do your ideal clients belong to? In other words, when are your ideal clients naturally in an audience?

A study conducted by the American Society of Association Executives found that seven out of ten Americans belong to at least one association. And one out of four has joined four or more associations! I know it's true that those living in other countries belong to numerous groups as well. These groups and associations are always on the lookout for speakers.

Determining organizations that would be likely to have your prospective clients or referral sources as members may take some digging. Ask those you work with what organizations they belong to or what meetings they attend. Are there any groups that you belong to where your target people are too? Ask friends, associates and mentors for suggestions on where you might speak. Visit the library or read your local newspaper, preferably your business paper, to see what organizations are in your community. And keep an eye out for seminars, workshops and classes that are offered throughout your community.

As you start to target possible groups, you might even call the membership chairperson or ask to attend a meeting just to scope out the territory. Find out if the group brings in speakers. Check to see if this is truly an audience you wish to target. Also, see if you can attend seminars offered by adult education institutions and business organizations.

Now that you have focused on your prospective clients, let's take a look at the myriad of places where you can present speeches and seminars to these folks. In Chapter 6, we'll take the steps to book these speaking engagements. Here are five dynamite areas where you can focus your talks.

1. ASSOCIATIONS, CIVIC GROUPS, COMMUNITY ORGANIZATIONS, RELIGIOUS GROUPS AND CLUBS

You may be utterly amazed as to how many organizations there really are out there. (Refer to the Resources Section in the Appendix for a sample list of groups.) If you live in a large city, your reference librarian may steer you to a local directory of business-related organizations.

Sometimes the local Chamber of Commerce can provide such a list. It may be worth buying a current edition of this listing if you think your prospective clients are members of this kind of group. If you are really lucky you can acquire these listings on disk, which will save a lot of data input when you start your correspondence.

While you are at the library, look up two gold-mine references: the *Encyclopedia of Associations* and the *National Trade and Professional Associations.* (See Resources in the Appendix for details.) Plan to spend some time thumbing through these huge volumes that list thousands of national and international

Whether your target clients are individuals, people in certain professions or decision-makers in particular companies, it is imperative that you know a lot about them.

organizations. You will get tons of ideas about all the associations that need speakers both for their local chapter meetings and for their larger conferences. Of course, your target right now is to speak at the local chapter level, but keep in mind that later you may find it advantageous to go all the way to the national or international level in your speaking. It's not uncommon for a local group, especially if prodded to do so, to recommend a speaker for their regional, national or international meetings. While you're researching various groups, make note of whether they have a newsletter or journal to which you can submit articles.

Keep your eyes open for meeting signs when you enter a local restaurant. Often the sign will have the group's logo and date and time the group meets at that restaurant. The manager can probably give you the name and phone number of the group's contact person or you can look them up in the phone book.

Check out the calendar of events section of your newspaper. You'll find many meetings listed there. These listings usually include the name of the organization, times and dates, as well of the speaker's topic. Guests are generally welcome.

Sometimes you'll even see posting of a group's meetings on community bulletin boards—both physical and virtual. Keep an eye out for such postings in your own neighborhood or in the communities where your prospects work or live. Go to areas on the Internet that your target prospects use.

Also check out your Yellow Pages under Associations, Business and Trade Organizations and Clubs.

It may be worth your while to join some of the groups and then offer to speak to them. Some organizations, especially chambers of commerce, have their own speakers bureau. This is a terrific way to get speaking gigs since many of the arrangements are made for you. Don't be intimidated if you'd like to join a professional group and you feel like an outsider. Many associations have a special membership bracket, often called associate, which may fit you to a tee. Remember, if your target clients belong, they need your services and it will be worth your feeling a bit like an outsider at first.

Please understand that I am not advocating that you ever join any group just to promote your business. Many organizations have been burned numerous times by moochers and they are quick to shun them. Make it clear that you are there to give as well as get. Volunteer to serve on a committee or do some needed task. The members will be watching and evaluating you. If they see that you are a person who follows through and adds value, you will have made some giant leaps in establishing trust and credibility, which in turn will lead to gaining clients.

For the vast majority of these organizations, a 20- to 30-minute speech is most desirable. Often it is given immediately after a meal is served. Occasionally these groups also have need for a longer seminar format. These can be 45-minute to an hour breakout sessions which are part of a convention or all-day conference.

2. PUBLIC SEMINARS SUCH AS ADULT EDUCATION CLASSES

The continuing education market is HOT and experts predict that it will continue to be so well into the 21st century. The Information Age is upon us. Adults are hungry for the latest information; they want you to share *your* expertise.

Because many adults choose to obtain this information through continuing education classes, they attend colleges, privately run schools, community centers, recreation centers or just about anywhere there is a classroom or meeting room. They love to attend classes at beautiful resorts, at retreats and on cruise ships. Also, many professionals are required to earn continuing education credits (CPE and CEUs), and consequently they are always searching for appropriate classes.

Pretend you are a detective hunting for adult education clues. You will be amazed at what you will suddenly start to see. The clues are all around you. A visit to your local library may reveal flyers and catalogs from community centers, recreational facilities and privately run adult education schools. Many of them are offering classes and they could be offering yours. Look in the neighborhoods close to community colleges and even grocery-store bulletin boards for class announcements. Check out small community newspapers: they often have a calendar section that lists upcoming classes offered all over town.

Open your telephone directory and check under Schools. Depending on the size of the community, there may be several community colleges as well as an adult education center. Check out recreation departments as well. Call these places and ask if there are any subjects that have been requested for which they have no instructor.

If you have friends and family in other cities, ask them to send you a copy of their local school's catalogs, or request them yourself. (See the addresses in the Resources Section of the Appendix.) Look for topics that are not (yet) offered in your town. You could be the trendsetter.

Adults are hungry for the latest information; they want you to share YOUR expertise.

Don't be discouraged if the topic you are considering is already being taught. You can create your own "spin" which will make it unique. (More on this in Chapters 2 and 3.) A consultant friend of mine wanted to teach telephone sales techniques but she found she had a lot of competition. So she designed her class to teach job seekers how to sell themselves over the phone. Believe me, she has created a winner!

Attend some continuing education classes so you can analyze the audience, the instructor and the material. Take notes on what you liked and what you would do differently.

The beauty of working with community colleges and adult education centers is that they do so much of the "grunt work" for you. They distribute their catalog throughout the community – an expense which would be astronomical for you. They provide the classroom and the audio-visual equipment. And sometimes they even assist with the cost of producing handouts. Many of the program coordinators can advise you about effective titles and course descriptions. They will also tell you which days of the week and times of day are best to offer your seminar. This is all a big help to a beginner. It will eliminate a lot of hassles and provide a shortcut on your path to success.

These types of seminars can range from as short as an hour to all day. You can decide to meet once or several times. In Chapter 14 you will find lots of ideas about how to convert your students in to clients.

Don't be surprised if a stranger wants to do business with you or refers business to you even if they did not take your class.

Here's a bonus: Don't be surprised if a stranger wants to do business with you or refers business to you even if they did not take your class. They assume you will serve them well just because you teach a class. And if the adult education institution does any publicity that's still another addition to your visibility quotient.

3. SELF-SPONSORED SEMINARS

Maybe your research on your ideal future clients reveals that they do not usually attend adult education classes but they may be drawn to a private seminar held in a nice hotel or resort. How about a cruise ship? Maybe you can offer them a meal, or at least some nice snacks and beverages.

If that's the case you may decide to "self-sponsor" a seminar. That's where you make all the arrangements and do all the promoting. The advantages? Well, you are in complete control. If you do your homework you'll probably draw a very targeted audience full of people who are ready to buy your services.

Many, many companies offer free seminars where they give a demonstration along with a sales presentation. Start looking for their advertisements in your newspaper and local magazines. You'll also hear this kind of event being promoted on radio and TV. Drop by and observe what they do.

But don't think you need to offer your self-sponsored seminar for free. In fact, your prospects may perceive a higher value if there is a fee for your seminar, rather than thinking all they will get is a high-pressure sales pitch. And if they shelled out money to hear you, they are probably some fairly serious prospects. It does tend to eliminate the curiosity seekers.

Let your imagination roll on this idea and you may come up with a collaborative effort with other professionals who wish to target the same group of buyers. How about a half-day conference on estate planning offered by a lawyer, a stockbroker, a CPA, an insurance agent and a CFP?

One great way to market your own seminar is by procuring a mailing list of your prospects and sending them a compelling invitation. We'll discuss very specific techniques for doing this in Chapter 7.

Another twist on this same theme is to give a seminar to your existing clients. This is an excellent way to acknowledge them, to inform them of recent trends and tell them about other services you can provide.

Self-sponsored seminars usually run anywhere from an hour to all day long.

4. SEMINARS SPONSORED BY SOMEONE ELSE

Maybe the thought of taking on that financial risk connected with self-sponsored seminars is a bit much for you right now. Well, a seminar sponsored by someone else may be just the ticket.

Let's just take a moment to brainstorm the possibilities of organizations you can ask to sponsor your presentation.

- Banks and credit unions
- Corporations offering events for their employees
- Cruise lines
- Department stores
- Employee assistance programs
- Hospitals and medical clinics
- Internet providers
- Malls and shopping centers
- Newspapers and magazines
- Office supplies stores
- Product suppliers
- Public libraries
- Resorts and tourist attractions
- Retirement homes
- Software companies
- Telephone companies
- Wineries and breweries

The list really is endless. Some of these entities are very accustomed to serving as a sponsor; others may need to be convinced. The nice thing about being sponsored by someone else is that they underwrite the costs, make all the arrangements and coordinate the promotion. Of course, you'll need to follow their guidelines.

Although most of these presentations are seminars, occasionally a company will sponsor a keynote speaker or a panel discussion. The vast majority of these presentations are in a seminar format lasting anywhere from 45 minutes to two hours. For example, it's not unusual for banks, office supply stores and software companies to put on a day of seminars for small business owners. This is a wonderful opportunity for lawyers, accountants, consultants and anyone else who targets that clientele.

5. TARGETING REFERRALS

Another variation on getting more clients through speaking is to solicit referrals from peers and collaborative professionals. In this case, you are shifting your target to colleagues who will recommend you to others.

Many professionals will not make referrals unless they know you or have seen you in action. Making a presentation to them is a wonderful way to show them your stuff. If you do a great job, the next time one of their clients or acquaintances needs your type of services, it's your name that comes to mind.

There is another strange phenomena that takes place once you start presenting to these types of groups. I call it the "prestige factor." You may find you'll get referrals from people who have never met you and have never even heard you speak. They assume that because you were on the agenda to speak to a particular group you are competent and dependable. Amazing, but just see if it doesn't happen to you. It's as if you have an invisible sales force (elves?) working for you.

Besides the organizations mentioned earlier, you may find these centers of influence at lead clubs and network groups.

Still another technique for getting referrals is to ask someone to attend one of your talks. Maybe it's an older professional in your own field who is no longer taking on new clients and would be glad to connect you with new people. Or it may be someone in a supporting profession.

2

DETERMINING YOUR BEST TOPICS

Your topics must pack a double-whammy. On the one hand, they must be something you would really enjoy talking about; and on the other hand, something your prospective clients and referral sources really want to hear about. In addition, the titles of your presentations and their descriptions must be very compelling.

Note: If the ideas in this chapter are new to you I suggest you read them over a number of times. Doing so will make a dramatic impact on not only your speaking success, but on your professional success as well.

DEVELOP A MISSION STATEMENT

Before you start to determine the topics you will speak on, it will be advantageous for you to develop a mission statement as to why you're giving these presentations and what you hope to accomplish. Yes, I know, the whole point is to gain more clients and referrals, but let's see how you do with the following questions:

- How will giving speeches and seminars position me in the market? Which market do I wish to target?
- Since speaking will establish me as an expert, just what kind of expert do I want to be perceived as? What will be my precise field of expertise?
- How will I go about establishing my credibility? Are there particular things I can consistently do to demonstrate my likability?

Making it clear why you are speaking is going to keep you on focus as you start to determine your topics.

Once you have a mission statement in place, the next step will be to develop goals for each presentation you make. Begin by asking yourself, Why am I speaking on this subject to this audience at this particular time?

Making it clear why you are speaking is going to keep you on focus as you start to determine your topics.

DETERMINE YOUR PROSPECTIVE CLIENTS' NEEDS

It may be tempting at this point of topic development to simply pick something that you find fascinating and run with it. But I'm going encourage you to slow down for a minute and switch the spotlight from your likes to your prospective clients' needs.

Let's imagine a set of binoculars that you are now using to zoom in on your target clients. Ask yourself the following:

- What do they want?
- What are they missing in their lives?
- What hurts?
- Where is the pain?
- What are they yearning for?
- What do they worry about most?

If you can provide the answers to these questions, you will start the process of meeting the needs of your clients and creating a winning presentation.

Here are a few ideas for gathering this type of information:

■ Conduct a survey. Ask your existing clients why they decided to work with you and what they think new clients would be interested in hearing about. Or survey the people you would love to have as clients—either on the phone, in person or on the Internet. Give them a choice of some possible topics they may want to hear more about or simply ask what are the things that get in the way of their success or happiness. If you hear something coming up time and time again, you've hit on a jackpot topic.

■ Check out the Internet chat sessions where your target clients might be involved. Find out what people are discussing. Jump in and offer a morsel of your expertise, then see what reaction you get. If they are asking for more, you've uncovered a hot topic.

■ Listen to those who predict growing trends in business and pick one. Some examples are aging baby boomers, cocooning, working mothers, etc. Play with ideas that incorporate a fit of your services with the latest demands of a trend. For example, a real estate agent or an architect may wish to focus on the space needs of those who run a business out of their home.

■ Pull out your professional journals and think about the newest developments in your field. Think about what subjects are being discussed at professional meetings you attend. Would your target population like to hear about these? Do they need to know how this new information will impact them? Tax accountants have a distinct advantage here since the government constantly supplies them with new material every time they decide to "simplify" the tax laws!

■ Take a look at current events. See if you can zero in on a subject that pops up often. Can you offer a new twist to a topic that all the talk shows are using?

■ Think back on what new acquaintances ask you about when at social gatherings. These are the folks who, once they hear what you do, attempt to get a bit of free advice. Don't bill them for it! Instead, consider it a favor, as they may have tipped you off on what could be a hot subject. One that may interest a lot of other folks, too.

DECIDE WHAT TOPICS YOU WOULD ENJOY

Okay, it's time to reverse those imaginary binoculars so their focus is on you. It is important that you also recognize what you really enjoy. Of the topics you have revealed so far, which would you enjoy talking about time and time again? You may come up with several subjects.

Caution! At this stage, there may be a strange human trait working against you. Many of us assume that just because we know a subject thoroughly, everyone else does too. We often take our own expertise for granted. Don't do that to yourself. Many people really want to learn what you know. They want you to share your passion with them.

It can also be tempting to force yourself to speak on a topic, even though you do not feel passionately about it. I do not recommend this. Sure, it might be a trendy topic for a while, but soon it will fade and then you are back to square one. It is much better to find a topic that you truly enjoy. You will be spending a lot of time developing your presentation, and hopefully you will be giving it for a long time. Make it worth your while. Remember, your audience will *always* know if you really care or if you are just going through the motions.

Many people really want to learn what you know. They want you to share your passion with them.

Let me share a story with you. I taught college accounting courses for several years and I reached the point where I had every lecture note memorized and knew every homework assignment inside-out. There were very few questions that my students could ask that I had not heard many, many times before. Had I not truly believed that accounting was extremely important to the success my students would experience in their lives and that the subject really could be fun, I would have been bored to tears. I can't claim that all my students ended up loving accounting, but they *did* learn it and they always commented on how my enthusiasm made it more enjoyable.

So pick a topic that really fits you, one that you love to talk about. And one that you will enjoy for years to come.

If you would like further help in developing your topic, check out the Topic Development Worksheet on the order form at the back of this book.

BENEFITS LEAD, FEATURES FOLLOW

Now that you have a pretty good idea of a topic or several topics you might wish to develop, let's gear our thinking to making those topics really work well.

If you have been in business for any length of time, you know that people buy benefits, not features. This notion can be a tremendous challenge to those of us who are highly educated, knowledgeable folks. Through our long schooling we were accustomed to stressing features (i.e., our degrees and certificates) rather than benefits. We may assume that people will come hear us speak just for the pure joy of becoming more informed. That's probably not so.

The other challenge is that we know so much. It is a formidable task to simplify it, get down to the basics and eliminate the jargon. We may be tempted to "data-dump" instead of keeping a narrow focus that is of interest to our audiences.

Still another challenge is that we may forget that what seems commonplace to us is new to others. Sometimes we are so immersed in our field we assume that everyone knows what we know. Not so.

The best way to surmount these challenges is to ruthlessly focus on benefits. Try this little exercise with a friend. Start by trying to convince him or her to attend your talk. With each reason you offer, ask your friend to reply, "Who cares?" As your conversation continues, you will get down to the one or two kernels of truth about why people will want to come hear you. These are the benefits you will sell.

WHAT BENEFITS ARE YOU OFFERING?

Unless your audience is chock full of hard-core academicians, your benefit can't be simply that they will gain new information. You must focus on how their lives will improve. There is a famous comment from a cosmetics executive who insisted he was not selling lipstick; what he was selling was hope. What are *you* selling?

> ***Take a look at why you are attracted to your topic and you'll discover facets that will also attract your future clients.***

You must be very clear about what people will gain from listening to you. How will your listeners' lives be better after hearing you? Will they have less stress? More peace of mind? A warm feeling that they have provided for their family? We are talking about emotions such as hope, fulfillment, inspiration, pride, etc. Take a look at why *you* are attracted to your topic and you'll discover facets that will also attract your future clients.

So why is it important to know this? You *must* know the benefits you are offering so you can sell them to the program planner and your future clients. (These are subjects we will discuss in Chapter 6.) And then everything you include in your presentation must be directed toward delivering this benefit or benefits to your audience.

YOUR PROMISE

Before you write your presentation, take a look at the promise you are making to your potential audience. This should be part of your talk's description and, ideally, also in your talk's title. (More on this later.) You *must* deliver what the presentation description promises. Your potential clients are asking the standard question, "What's in it for me?" They need to be assured that they are making a wise decision and that you will deliver on your promise.

If you spend your entire time promoting your business and not giving any tangible value, your audience will feel ripped off (rightly so), and you will have created a negative image.

As you design the presentation, keep your focus in mind. Your focus is what the listener should be able to have, be or do, as a result of hearing you. If an item doesn't meet the objective, improve it, throw it out or, better yet, save it in a file folder for a possible future presentation.

It's essential that you keep the promises you are making, so be realistic about what you can accomplish in a very short time.

SHOOTING FOR YOUR GOALS

Of course, besides the value you plan to deliver in your talk, you also want to sell yourself and your services. Be prepared to tell your audience why they should use your services now. Folks in the investment industry have a distinct advantage here. They can always bring in the time value of money, and mention such zingers as, "Well, if you had invested $100 with me five years ago you would have this huge amount now."

Be prepared to tell your audience why they should use your services now.

If you think it is going to become a deciding factor for your clients, be ready to state why they should work with you and not your competition.

There are lots of ideas for selling from the platform in Chapter 8.

DEVELOP A CATCHY TITLE

A title with a hook or built-in benefit is the best. Make sure it grabs attention and promises value. Someone once said, "You gotta have a gimmick!" And it is so true!

Start with this formula and fill in the blanks: How to _____ so that you can _____ (this will be the benefit of attending). Here are some examples:

How to ***Qualify for Tax Exemptions***
So That You Can ***Save Hundreds of Dollars***

How to ***Save an Hour a Day***
So That You Can ***Have More Time With Your Family***

How to ***Take Care of Your Survivors***
So That You Can ***Have Peace of Mind Today***

Eventually some of the formula words fall out. You may drop the words "how to."

Reduce the Cost and Hassle of Buying Your Next Home

Sometimes the phrase "so that you can" ends up in an adjective or adverb.

Fund Your Child's College Education ***Effortlessly***

When you let your creative juices flow, all sorts of ideas will emerge. Here are some excellent examples:

Ten Fatal Financial Mistakes and How to Avoid Them

Live Debt-Free—For Life!

How to Negotiate with Anyone, Anywhere, Anytime

Eat Your Way to Good Health

Sometimes it works to sound controversial. How about . . .

Spend Your Retirement Now

Bankruptcy Should Be Outlawed

The Value of Stress

Avoid what I call "Miss Universe statements." Meaningless, vague words that say nothing—"Invest in the Future Today" (ho-hum), or "Plan a Great Career" (yawn time). Be more specific and be clear on the value your listeners will receive.

WRITE UP A COMPELLING DESCRIPTION OF YOUR TALK

If you are sponsoring your own seminar you will absolutely need a description that will compel people to attend—whether it is free or not. It's also very possible that a meeting planner or a seminar sponsor will ask for a description of your talk. Sometimes they even limit you to a word count.

One outstanding way to sell value and to keep yourself on track is to structure your topic into some sort of formula, such as Seven Steps, or Ten Points or Three Secrets. The reader then feels assured that they will walk away with something of value—practical, specific information, rather than just a general theoretical discussion.

Study other descriptions of seminars and classes and emulate the ones that make you want to attend.

As much as possible, use lively words such as discover, learn, enjoy, discuss. List the specific skills, strategies, tips, techniques and measurable results the participants will receive from your presentation. Build in some urgency to take action now.

Personalize your description by using the word "you" instead of "the participant."

And if it's a technical subject, assure the reader that the material will be easy to understand.

After you have written your description, test it by asking, Would someone take a day off work to hear this topic? Or drive 30 grueling miles in rush hour to find out more? If not, keep rewriting until you have something that really draws people. Ask the meeting planner or seminar sponsor for their input, too.

SEMINAR LEADERS NEED TO COMPOSE A "THOSE WHO SHOULD ATTEND" SECTION

Seminar brochures often have a section called "Who Should Attend." If written well, this will really help you prequalify the people who come to your seminar. For example, if your topic is geared for small business owners, say so and save those who will not be interested a lot of time and frustration.

After you've written your description, test it by asking, Would someone take a day off work to hear this topic?

3

TIPS ON DESIGNING SUCCESSFUL PRESENTATIONS

It is essential that you design your presentation so you achieve your goals and the folks in your audience feel they have received value. Also, what you design may very well become a referral fountain that gushes forth over and over again. It will be well worth your time to design a geyser.

Note: This is a general chapter about presentation design. In the next two chapters we will focus on specific formats for a speech and a seminar.

SET GOALS FOR EACH AND EVERY PRESENTATION

You will get the most benefit out of giving speeches and seminars if you set goals. Determine the goals that will work best for you. As you give more and more speeches and seminars, you will become more precise about the goals you set. The most meaningful goals are those that are very specific, such as: "At this presentation, I will collect business cards from over 75% of the audience. I will contact these people within 48 hours and I will convert 30% of them to clients." Of course, if you establish goals you must also set up some sort of tracking system to see if you accomplish them. You'll also want to analyze what went wrong if you did not meet your goals and how you can improve next time. In Chapter 8 we'll look at how to methodically plan when and how to make your "sales pitch" during your presentation.

ATTEND OTHER SPEECHES AND SEMINARS

As you begin to think about the format of your own presentations, you'll receive a great deal of value by observing others. Seek out those in your own field or in completely different fields who are making presentations. Attend and observe them at two levels:

1. Note the content of the presentation. Did it seem to follow a particular formula? What techniques did the presenter use to make the material interesting?

2. Note the presenter's style. Did they use a question-and-answer period? Were the visual aids effective? Did the humor work?

Watch and talk to the audience about their reactions. Give some thought to what you liked and did not like about the presentation. Bottom-line questions are: Would you want to do business with or refer people to this speaker? Did you trust them? If not, why not?

USE MIND MAPS AND OTHER CREATIVE TECHNIQUES TO COMPOSE THE CONTENTS OF YOUR TALK

A mind map captures on paper all the thoughts you might have about a particular subject. Start by writing your topic in the center of a large piece of paper and then drawing a circle around it. As you think of points you want to include, place them radiating out from the center topic. If you use lots of colors and pictures, your creative juices will start flowing. On one piece of paper you will have captured all the points you'll want to make on a particular subject.

Often creative ideas seem to fly into our heads at very odd moments—in the shower, while driving or watching TV. Start gathering these treasures by recording them on a cassette, in a notepad or in a file folder that is specifically devoted to presentation ideas.

You will get the most benefit out of giving speeches and seminars if you set goals.

BALANCE YOUR NEED TO CREATE VALUE WITH NOT GIVING AWAY THE WHOLE SHOW

Beginning presenters often data dump. We know so much about our subject that we think we must share *everything* we know. This may also come from a desire to impress people with our expertise. Presenting too much material will turn your audience off quickly. Keep condensing your information down to the bare essentials. Leave your audience thirsty for more.

It might help to imagine holding onto a laser sword and cutting out anything that does not directly relate to your main message. Yes, I know it is tempting to include a cute story or joke you just heard. But if it does not directly relate to your points, you'll only confuse people and give them the impression that you really don't have your act together. Be ruthless. But do save those dissected gems—they may work well in the next presentation you design.

MAKE YOUR OPENING AND CONCLUSION WORK FOR YOU

♦ FIRST, YOUR CONCLUSION

As strange as it may seem, it is best if you write your last words first. Your conclusion is your chance to summarize what you've said and ask for what you want. Doing so will help you reach the goals you've set for your talk.

> ***The first few words must grab your audience's attention and persuade them to listen to you.***

Select one of the following techniques:

- A summary of your points
- An appeal to action
- A story that illustrates your message
- A powerful quotation

Your conclusion should tie back to something you said in your opening. This gives everyone a sense of completion and a signal that you are wrapping it up.

End on a happy note. If you enjoyed being with your audience, tell them so sincerely. Thank them for their time and attention. They will be flattered and responsive. Be sure to make it clear how they can contact you and what their next step should be.

It's very wise to write out your conclusion word for word and memorize it. It is that important.

◆ THEN YOUR OPENING

The first few words that come out of your month are key to the rest of your presentation. They must grab your audience's attention and persuade them to listen to you. It's possible that many members of your audience are still thinking about a problem at work, the terrible commute they just had or a pressing family matter. You must bring their attention to you and your message. Here are some effective techniques for doing just that. Select one for your opening.

- A challenging statement
- A startling question (but avoid trite ones like, "How many of you would like a million dollars?" Your goal is to get them to start thinking about your topic. Phrase your question so it can be answered with a yes or no.)
- A dramatic quotation
- A story that relates to your message
- An impressive fact
- A dynamite joke (just be sure it is appropriate and relates to your topic)

Now that you have their attention, you'll need to convince them of the benefits they will receive from listening to you. I know, they are already there listening, but are they really? You must convince them they will receive value. We adults are a funny lot. Most of us are very sensitive about appearing foolish. Reassure your audience that they did not make a mistake in attending your workshop, because you will never put a participant on the spot. Work hard to create a positive and supportive environment so that learning can happen.

If an introducer has not established your credentials, you will need to mention them early in your presentation so that your listeners know you are qualified to speak on your subject.

From here it is wise to give them a preview of where you are going. You might say something like, "Let's look at three steps to . . ."

Since you may be nervous at the beginning of your presentation, it's best to be very familiar with your opening. Practice it over and over again. Don't be tempted to change it at the last moment. It's best to start out strong, confident and enthusiastic.

ADDING INTEREST

Today's audiences are accustomed to a fast-changing pace. It is imperative that you plan to re-grab their attention every three to five minutes. There are many ways to add interest to your presentation and avoid becoming just a "talking head." Plan to use at least one of the following techniques for each point you make in your talk.

◆ STORIES/ANECDOTES

It is amazing to me how often I can remember a story I heard and its effect on me, although I've forgotten the facts that were presented at the same time. Stories are very effective tools for learning because they engage our emotions as well as our logic.

Now here's a challenge for you. Practice until you can recite your story by heart and still sound spontaneous. Think of how many times a great singer performs the same popular song. Be sure to give your story the same amount of passion and freshness as you did the first time you told it.

Caution: Be sure that your story is something the audience will be able to connect with. I once listened to a speaker who used football stories for every example he gave. I do not like football and know little about the game. And I sensed that was also true of others in the audience. In essence, he was teaching us to stop listening to him and we quickly complied. Taking care that your audience will be able to relate to your story is especially important if you have people from other countries or with a very different background from yours.

Here's an excellent way for you to establish your expertise. Tell (brag?) about one of your client's successes. People love to hear this type of story. It will paint you as a bit of a hero who saved the day for a client. But what people are also hearing is that you were the key ingredient in that success. Your

Today's audiences are accustomed to a fast-changing pace.

audience may well conclude that you have the recipe for *their* future success. It is usually best to keep your former client's name anonymous, but do give specific data about the accomplishment. For example, a financial planner may explain how she saved a client several hundred dollars in taxes by setting up an IRA (a retirement investment).

Stories are a wonderful way for you to reveal your passion about your subject and commitment to helping others. Start keeping a collection of stories, both yours and others', that you can use in your presentations. Here's an added bonus: If you are having one of those days when nothing seems to go right, pull out your success stories collection. A good read will often get you right back on track.

Remember, besides providing others with information, it is important that we entertain them as well. Stories do just that for us. They touch our emotions. They are also a lovely way to show our sense of humor and share a laugh. Of course, all your stories need not be funny. Just be sure that they relate to and strengthen the point you are making.

◆ ANALOGIES/COMPARISONS

Adults tend to learn by associating new material that they are trying to learn with what they already know. Give them a hand by making comparisons such as, "A computer's CPU is like a human's brain the monitor is like a TV; the keyboard is like a typewriter." Using analogies and comparisons is a effective way to cement new ideas into your audience's mind.

◆ STATISTICS

These consist of numbers, percentages and dollar amounts that support your point. It works best to compare your facts with something your audience can comprehend; for example, such-and-such is as high as a ten-story building. Visual aids can be very effective here. You can let your audience see the numbers while you are stating them, and use charts and graphs to help illustrate your statistics. You can also aid comprehension by rounding off numbers like 5,974 to "about 6,000." Be sure not to overwhelm your audience with too many numbers. Be choosy and make sure they support your point.

◆ CASE STUDIES

Using an example of how a typical family or typical client could use your recommendations to improve their lives is an excellent way to bring your material down to earth. Your case should closely parallel your typical audience member so that they can easily relate to it. It is dramatic to set up two scenarios for your case study. One is the doom-and-gloom picture of what happened because they did not follow your advice. And, of course, the second shows how their lives were enriched by working with you.

◆ QUOTATIONS

Quotations are an excellent way to add some variety to your talk. But don't get carried away. Avoid using lengthy quotes. And don't use too many. Remember, your audience came to hear you and your own ideas. Practice the quotation several times so you are comfortable saying it. And be sure you have the complete wording in your notes. Always give credit to the originator of the quotation, if possible. Avoid saying, "quote . . . unquote," or drawing the quote marks in the air with your fingers. It looks amateurish and is very distracting. The spectators will love it if you quote a leader of their group who is in the audience.

◆ PROPS AND VISUAL AIDS

This is an outstanding way to get your ideas to "stick." Chapter 10 offers many ideas on using props and visual aids.

But it's a useful idea to start thinking what aids you will use as you design your presentation.

◆ AUDIENCE PARTICIPATION

Even if your presentation is as short as 20 to 30 minutes it is worth your while to take the time to get your audience involved. This can be as simple as asking them some "getting-to-know-you" questions at the beginning. Another technique is asking them to complete an exercise included in their handout and then encouraging them to discuss it. Small group exercises and discussions are also effective but can take up a lot of time. Plan to use them in longer seminars when you have more time.

◆ USE HUMOR

You're in the business of entertaining as well as informing. Use humor but don't be offensive. Better to tell a joke on yourself. One gag I use in just about every seminar concerns my poor spelling. It's something I can't hide when I use a chalkboard or flip chart, so I spell common words in very creative ways—ruff draft, thruout, succe$$ful, etc. Then with a big smile, I explain that I can spell some words as many as five different ways, and that it really is a sign of creative genius. About half of the audience (the other poor spellers) agrees with me and we share a good laugh. Next, I show them how I could tell when my college professors couldn't spell and I scribble a word on the board so that nobody can tell what letters I used. I exclaim that it still works for doctors—just try to read your next perscription—oops, prescription!

Write out your jokes and include them in your notes. You may think you have them memorized but it is amazing how quickly they can vaporize when you're in front of an audience.

The following subjects will be discussed in depth in upcoming chapters but it is also important to consider them in the design process.

PREPARE YOUR NOTES SO THAT THEY ARE USEFUL TO YOU

I would *not* suggest that you just "wing" your presentation, even if you feel you know your material well. Preparing an outline will guarantee that you don't miss any points and will keep you on track. Your notes need not follow a strict, formal outline format. Several speakers I know use various colors and pictures in their notes to remind them of the points they plan to cover. By preparing effective notes your audience will get what they came for.

Some speakers put their notes on index cards. These are easy to carry and are less obvious to the audience, but they can get a bit bulky if you are presenting a seminar that will last several hours. One big advantage of putting your material on index cards is the ease of rearrangement. For example, if you decide you will not have time for one of your points, you can easily eliminate those related cards from your pile. Or you can rearrange the order. Of course, you do not want to rearrange your order by dropping the whole pile on the floor as I once did moments before a presentation. I have always numbered my cards ever since!

The majority of seminar presenters keep their notes in a three-ring binder and do not let it out of their sight. That means they put it in their carry-on luggage when flying because they know they would be lost without it. A binder gives you the flexibility of moving things around and deleting sections when you are pressed for time. Leave the left side

Preparing an outline will guarantee that you don't miss any points and will keep you on track. By preparing effective notes your audience will get what they came for.

page blank so that you can make notes as you are speaking or immediately afterward. This is a very useful way to keep revising your presentation. Who knows, this could easily lead to a published book.

The major problem with notes is that it's tempting to overuse them. Never just stand and read from your notes—nothing will put your audience to sleep faster. Your notes should not reflect every single word you intend to say, but rather provide an outline of the main points and cues as to when to insert a favorite story or example. I even include some of those trite smiley-face stickers on the first few pages of my notes, to remind me when I'm most nervous to smile and have fun while I'm presenting.

KEEP YOUR PRESENTATION ON TIME

They say that in effective humor, timing is everything. It's also essential in an effective presentation. You will lose your audience if you run overtime! And your listeners will be annoyed by this disruption to their schedules. If you end your presentation on time or even a little early you will gain many points with your audience and bonus points with a meeting planner. The trick is to stop speaking before they stop listening!

Here are very effective-fail tips that will keep you on time, every time:

- First, practice your presentation so that it runs the designated length. Time yourself several times. Write down in your notes the time it should be when you reach each point. Allow time for laughter and other audience reactions. Tell folks how much time they will have for the question-and-answer period. And keep them on task.

- Secondly, use 'fudge paragraphs.' These are examples, stories and thoughts that can be included if you need to fill in time or eliminated if you need to speed up. Always be prepared to give a lot more content than you think the time allows; then you're ready to fill in at a moment's notice.

- Last, be sure that you know exactly what time it is at every moment. Check to see if there is a clock hanging in the room, wear a watch you can read easily or bring a small, easy-to-read travel clock that you can set on the podium.

THINKING ABOUT AV

As you plan your presentation, it's a good idea to start thinking about which audio-visual aids would best help you make your points.

Develop a back-up presentation in case something happens to your visual aids. For instance, if your original presentation is dependent on using the overhead projector, be ready to also present it using a flip chart or chalkboard.

MAKING YOUR PITCH

> ***It is important that you plan how and when you will include your self-promotion.***

Think about how and when you will make your sales pitch during your presentation. You don't want to oversell, yet it is important that you plan to include your self-promotion. Usually it works best at the end of your presentation, when people will remember it best then.

PLAN FOR A QUESTION-AND-ANSWER SESSION

Sometimes this type of interaction with the audience is just not feasible. But if it is possible, determine whether you want questions asked at the end of each point and/or at the end of your presentation. Let the participants know when it is appropriate to ask questions. Adults need this opportunity to relate your material directly to their own situations.

GIVE OUT HANDOUTS

It's useless to make a presentation without giving out a handout—even if it is only your business card. And hopefully it will be much more. Start thinking about the most important things you want people to walk away with and remember.

You may want to provide a glossary in your handout if it is important that your listeners understand the meaning of certain terms. (But be sure not use too much jargon. It will only confuse your audience.)

4

CREATING A POPULAR SPEECH

Now that we have examined some general design principles in the last chapter, it's time to focus on speeches. Once you have designed a great speech you can use it over and over again. You may find that giving speeches to your prospective clients or to possible referral sources becomes your best source of new clients. And you may discover that you thoroughly enjoy sharing your information with others.

WHAT'S MOST IN DEMAND

The majority of the freebie speeches are given to associations, civic groups and community organizations. The most requested length is 20 to 30 minutes. Once your availability is known, you may be asked to serve as a guest on a panel discussion. Also, it's possible that you'll have the opportunity to present a 50- to 60-minute keynote speech sponsored by someone else.

THE OLD RELIABLE "THREE MAIN POINTS" FORMULA

Once you start observing other speakers, you'll recognize that the "three main points" formula is used over and over again. Why? Because it is simple and it works.

Outline what you want to say by following this basic formula:

- Opening
- Point 1 (simplest)

  Interesting support for Point 1

- Point 2
  Interesting support for Point 2
- Point 3 (more complex)
  Interesting support for Point 3
- Conclusion

If your speech is longer than 30 minutes, go ahead and add one or two more points. But don't try to cram lots of points into a short time. You'll feel rushed and your listeners will be overwhelmed.

If you think designing your speech would be easier by completing fill-in-the-blank worksheets, refer to the order form at the back of this book.

ANOTHER SPEECH FORMULA THAT MAY ALSO WORK WELL FOR YOU

The "problem-solution formula" also works well in promoting your services. You are the solution to their problems, of course!

First, state the problem. Describe it in graphic terms so your listeners are sure you thoroughly understand it. Acknowledge that perhaps many of them are experiencing such an issue.

Next, anticipate any objections and offer possible solutions. You may choose to first discuss alternative solutions (your competitor's?) and then demonstrate why your solution is better. Case studies, examples and stories will help illustrate how people's lives are improved after following your solution. Remember, most of us buy on emotion and rationalize the decision with logic. Be sure to supply more than facts. Give them an emotional appeal as well.

Finally, call for action on their part. The assumption is that since you offer the best solution to their problem, they need to know the next step to take to start working with you.

Again, refer to the Designing Your Speech Worksheets on the order form at the back of this book.

GETTING YOUR POINT ACROSS WHEN YOU'RE ON A PANEL

Sometimes panel discussions are very well organized and you have an opportunity to make a well-prepared presentation. It's ideal when the moderator provides each member with a list of discussion questions beforehand. Even though you will be sharing the spotlight with others and you may not have much time to speak, it is best to be prepared. Often when panel members decide to wing it, they stray way off the topic and go on too long. As a result, the listeners go away disappointed.

If your panel leader does not share the agenda with you, try to anticipate what will be asked and how you will respond. Stories and examples work well here as long as they are short and to the point. Try to think of something you can do or say that will make you memorable—in a positive way, of course. If the leader did not introduce you properly, briefly tell the audience why you are qualified to speak on the subject. If the discussion is running out of time before you've had an opportunity to speak, give an abbreviated version of your presentation and offer to stay afterward to speak to people.

Take the time to get to know the other members of the panel. They could end up being some of your best referral sources. Be ready to distribute your business cards or offer a free give-away after the discussion ends.

ACKNOWLEDGE YOUR INTRODUCER AND THE AUDIENCE

Be courteous and thank your introducer when you begin your speech. If it seems appropriate, shake their hand as you approach the podium. If you provide a written introduction (more on that in Chapter 9) and they botch it, you'll probably be disappointed. Just make the best of the situation and never criticize them in front of others. Sometimes introducers ramble on or do little to make the audience excited to listen to you. This will be a test of your patience and professionalism. Your enthusiasm and a powerful, well-rehearsed opening will overcome any initial negativity.

Your enthusiasm and a powerful, well-rehearsed opening are essential.

One of the best things you can do to endear yourself to your audience is to flatter them by finding something out about them. You can get this type of information from your contact person or by reading literature about the group. For example, if the group just completed a successful fundraising event, compliment them on their efforts and tell them what an honor it is to address such a hard-working group. This will show people that you are willing to go the extra mile. By doing this, you will establish yourself as an insider who really understands them.

A caution needs to be expressed here. Avoid being trite and insincere. Many audiences are turned off by preliminary mushiness and would prefer that the speaker jump right into a stimulating opening. If you sense that is true about the group you are to address, don't disappoint them.

WHAT TO DO IMMEDIATELY AFTERWARDS

Your marketing efforts are not over when you spout the last words of the speech. In fact, often the real work has just begun. Give some thought as to what you will do immediately after your speech. No, not run out the door in sweet relief! The group's agenda will dictate most of this. Will the audience be able to approach you immediately afterwards? Do you plan to move into the audience and collect business cards or deliver a promotional gift? Will you quickly move to the back of the room to stand by your display table?

> ***Your marketing efforts are not over when you spout the last words of the speech. In fact, often the real work has just begun.***

If you've done a great job, many people will want to talk to you. But it is important that you don't let one person dominate your time while others grow impatient and maybe even leave. Be assertive with a non-stop talker. Point out to them that others are waiting. Suggest that you talk at length at a more convenient time—either you will call them or invite them to call you. There may be times when you need to repeat your request several times before they get it. But always be courteous. Others in line will be watching you and, although they are anxious for their turn, they also want to be sure that everyone is treated well too.

Sometimes having several conversations, one right after another, can be mind-boggling. Especially if you are straining to remember names, faces and the details of the discussion. Here's a technique that works well. Take that person's business card and write key words on the back. For instance, if you promised to send them a brochure, write the word "brochure" on the card. Then, when you get back to your office, you can easily associate that person's name and the content of your conversation.

FOCUS ON ONE OR TWO SPECTACULAR SPEECHES

It may be tempting to write a brand-new speech for every gig you get, but don't do it. It's far too time-consuming. And once you design one or two solid speeches, you can use them over and over again. It is nice to give a meeting planner a choice of a couple speeches—just don't get carried away.

Oh sure, it's nice to try out a new visual aid. Or a new joke. But don't change more than 10% of your speech each time. You'll be less nervous giving a speech with which you are very familiar.

What you can do is customize your core speech to meet the needs of each audience. Substitute a story or example that more aptly applies to that group. For example, a health practitioner who speaks on stress reduction may talk to working women about time management whereas an audience of retirees may want to hear more about staying active.

Once you design one or two solid speeches, you can use them over and over again.

This isn't to imply that you should not be constantly improving and updating your speech. If a joke bombed the last two times, it's time to find another one. If the same question is asked over and over again, it's time to incorporate the answer into your speech. Continually fine-tuning your speech will produce better results and also keep you enthusiastic about the material.

It is possible that a few people may hear your same "core speech" twice. Not to worry. Think of how many times you have heard your favorite comedian's routines. If it's a good speech they'll enjoy it again, and many won't remember all of your points anyway.

5

BUILDING A VALUABLE SEMINAR

Because so many of us have attended a gazillion seminars, designing one is really second nature. Plus you may find that you enjoy presenting seminars and interacting with the participants. You'll marvel at the uniqueness of each group. And you may even find yourself joyfully anticipating your next seminar.

DEFINING SEMINARS AND MORE

These days the words "seminar" and "workshop" are often used interchangeably. Technically, the word "workshop" implies that the participants will be more actively involved. But many of us have sat through a very long "workshop" where we became extremely bored statues. You may choose to call your presentation a seminar, workshop, class, clinic, training session, demonstration, break-out session or whatever. Just be sure to study your market and find out what your clients expect.

The term "seminar" is also used to describe an all-day event consisting of several presentations. These affairs can also be referred to as conventions or conferences. And they can last for several days.

You can see that if you are working with a meeting planner it would be worth your while to clarify exactly how they interpret these terms.

WHAT'S MOST IN DEMAND

Aim for either a 45- to 50-minute seminar or a two-hour session with a break in the middle. Remember, there are a number of ways to go with this. It could be public seminar, self-sponsored or sponsored by someone else. And you could be speaking directly to your prospective clients or to possible referral sources.

MODULES WORK WELL

One of the best ways to design a seminar is to build stand-alone modules for each of your subtopics or points. Many times these can be interchangeable or can even grow into a spin-off seminar. The length of each module can then be very flexible depending on the schedule or needs of the participants.

Modules do very well with topics like "Five Reasons to . . . "Seven Mistakes and How to Avoid Them." Yes, it is simplistic and it works. It works because it is so easy. This format is easy for your audience to understand, follow where you are going and remember afterwards. It is easy for you because it forces you to keep the material focused and condensed.

Sometimes your subtopics will not be so interchangeable. For instance, perhaps your topic lends itself more to a chronological order or a linear sequence, such as "Seven Steps to Preparing a Painless Tax Return" or "The Procedures for Filing for Bankruptcy." Still, developing a module for each point will produce a great presentation.

Each module should have interesting support material and may also include some sort of group participation.

It is essential that you present solid, practical and timely information. It needs to be real "nuts-and-bolts" information that adults can use immediately.

> ***One of the best ways to design a seminar is to build stand-alone modules for each of your subtopics. Often these can be interchangeable or even developed into a spin-off seminar.***

Inexperienced presenters often give far too much information, so go back and whittle down your outline even more. No data dumping.

It's easy to create your seminars using the fill-in-the-blank Designing Your Seminar Worksheet. See order form at the back of this book for details.

ICE-BREAKERS ARE OFTEN WORTH THE TIME

Ice-breakers, such as having each person introduce themselves, can gobble up an enormous amount of time but they are often worth it. If you have only 45 minutes and more than 20 people, your ice-breaker could take up all your time. But if you have either a smaller group or more time, plan on doing some kind of ice-breaker.

If you have people introduce themselves you might also ask them to say what they would most like to get out of your time together. It's an excellent way to find out your prospective clients' most pressing needs. Then, tailor your seminar to meet their requests or suggest that you talk with them privately later. Also, when people introduce themselves, listen intensely and try to memorize names. Your audience will be flattered and it really shows that you have every intention of working with them further.

> ***Effective ice-breakers can ease tension and build camaraderie.***

After a lunch break or a long day, ice-breakers that encompass physical activity, such as walking around the room and talking to people, are wonderful for increasing the energy level.

Effective ice-breakers also have a way of easing any tension and of building some camaraderie. This will work in your favor especially if you will be talking about touchy subjects such as death, taxes, divorce, illness, etc. Another format is to have each person introduce themselves to the stranger sitting next to them, and prep them to ask each other some thought-provoking question on your topic that you provide. This will help everyone to focus immediately and it reduces any sense of isolation.

GROUP PARTICIPATION EXERCISES SAVE THE DAY

Adults sometimes like to be active in the learning process, so group exercises or case studies work well. If you signed up for a cooking class, wouldn't you like to actually mix up some ingredients rather than listen to someone lecturing you about the process?

Strategically placed group exercises will give your audience a break from constantly listening and an opportunity to assimilate your information. Nobody learns well from long lectures, so plan to break up your material frequently.

Group exercises also can give you a well-deserved break. Rest your voice and body. This should include sitting down for a while. You'll find you will do a better job of presenting if you take care of yourself.

Typical group participation exercises are:

- Writing in the handout
- Small-group discussions
- Brainstorming
- Case studies

THE VALUE OF BREAKS

It's funny, but the more I present workshops and speeches, the more convinced I am of the importance of breaks and the time after the presentation. Don't be fooled. This is not a time for *you* to relax. This is the time when the most important work takes place. It is the time to sharpen your listening skills.

People will often approach you with private questions and comments. You must listen carefully and answer them fully. But you can't let one person monopolize you. Breaks during long presentations are also important to give the learner some time to move around and let the information soak in. Adults also enjoy the social interaction during the breaks.

Consider giving a break assignment such as "Find three people who…" or "Test out your new approach on four new people." This encourages people to mingle and network. Sometimes people just need an excuse to strike up a conversation.

While the people are in the restrooms, they may be saying what a great person you are. At least, we hope so! If your presentation runs for more than one hour, plan to give your audience a well-deserved break.

WHY YOU MAY WISH TO PROVIDE FOOD AND BEVERAGES

Offering food shows the participants that you are sensitive to their needs. The promise of hot coffee and rolls may be just the incentive they need in the morning to make an effort to come hear you. Or the assurance of beverages and nibbles after a long, hectic workday may lessen the temptation to bag your seminar and head straight home. Eating together often relaxes people and encourages social connections. They start associating you with a pleasant time.

BEGINNINGS

Besides a really enthusiastic opening as we discussed in Chapter 3, seminars demand more at the beginning. Because seminars usually run much longer than a speech, participants need to be reassured about the structure. Early on, let them know when the breaks will be and where the restrooms and phones are located.

Your opening remarks need to include your credentials and the value the audience will receive by participating in your seminar.

Share with them any "rules"—such as when to ask questions, if it's okay to help themselves to beverages, etc.—so they are comfortable with the set-up.

Most seminar leaders do not have someone to introduce them, so you must act as the host and warm up the audience to hearing you. Your opening remarks need to include your credentials and the value the audience will receive by participating in your seminar.

WHAT TO DO IMMEDIATELY AFTERWARDS

Plan to stick around after your seminar to talk with participants. For many this is their next step to hiring you. Be sure to listen intently and answer their questions thoroughly.

If several people are lined up to speak with you, keep the line moving. Ask those who have a lot to share or continue to ask questions if you can continue your conversation over coffee later or on the telephone the next day.

6

BOOKING AS MANY SPEAKING GIGS AS YOU WANT

Now that you have designed a dynamite presentation (or two) and thought about where to find your ideal clients naturally in an audience, the next step is to get some speaking gigs on your calendar. In this chapter we will look at several things you can do to book gigs—whether someone else is setting up the arrangements or you are sponsoring your own programs.

PREP WORK

Before you start to make contact with meeting planners it is imperative that you do your homework. Become crystal-clear as to the reasons they should book you. Also, formulate reasons why this is the perfect topic for this group. Again, as we did in Chapter 2, focus on the audience and what they will gain by listening to you. But also broaden your focus to include the event planner and their needs. Anything you can do to make the planner look good would be to your benefit. They are taking a bit of a risk on you, an unknown. Assure them that you will do a professional job and do nothing to embarrass them or make them regret that they booked you.

Much of this reassurance comes across in the manner with which you present yourself both orally and in writing. Always speak in a confident manner and be absolutely sure that your written material—letters, forms, flyers—look very professional. I know: acting confident, especially the first couple of times you talk to these folks, may be a bit of a stretch. Just remember the old adage, "Act as if." Pretend that you have already made dozens of these presentations and even received standing ovations. Doing this homework before you sell to the meeting planners will also boost your confidence level.

Prepare a faxable flyer about your presentations. It should include the title and a description that emphasizes the value the audience will receive. It needs to also include a brief biography about you and why you are qualified to speak on this subject. Include things like your training and number of years in your field, etc. Very often a meeting planner needs this type of information immediately, or even yesterday, and will greatly appreciate that it is all ready to be faxed or e-mailed to them.

Before contacting meeting planners it is imperative that you are crystal-clear about why they should book you.

MAKING CONTACT

First, be sure to review the numerous groups you can give your talks to (discussed in Chapter 1). Whether your initial contact is by letter or by phone really depends on your preference and the circumstances. If you got someone's name and number through your networking efforts, then it probably makes more sense to call first. If you are targeting a list of local associations and community groups, then it may be better to write a form letter. See the offer-to-speak letter in Examples Section of the Appendix. Be sure to use professional stationery. And check to make sure you spell the contact person's name correctly.

Often the group's program planner is a volunteer member. These folks are often desperate to fill up the speaking slots for the entire year. (Perhaps you have even served in this role.)

If you wish to teach in an educational institution, call and ask what their procedure is for proposing a class. Sometimes they will want you to fill out one of their forms. Be sensitive to the fact that you may have called at a busy time, i.e., registration week, and offer to call back later.

You will also want to find out what their timelines are. Many institutions must book their events as much as a year in advance, in order to have their catalog printed and distributed in time. Before you write your proposal, spend some time analyzing the sponsoring organization's other offerings. Will your seminar fit in? Do they seem to be targeting the same people you wish to have in your audience? You should also prepare a class outline, in case the sponsor wishes to review the course contents. Proposals can be as short as a paragraph or as long as several pages. Ask them how much information they need.

Many years ago, when I wrote my very first proposal, I was fortunate enough to have several years' worth of catalogs to study. I saw how some courses were dropped after only one listing. I didn't want that to happen to me, so I modeled my description after the ones that were repeated year after year. I knew that they were the winners.

Remember that you not only have to sell your potential audience on the value of your talk, but you must also sell the sponsoring organization. You must convince them that you have a "bestseller." The more research you do, the better. Be prepared to show how your topic is part of a current trend or why people are eager for this information. Don't be discouraged if your analysis reveals that someone else is already offering a class of your topic. You may still get in if you can

Not only do you need to sell your potential audience on the value of your talk, you must also sell the sponsoring organization.

offer a different angle or cater to another niche audience. Remember, there is a lot of turnover in this field. A presenter may have left and the institution may be desperately looking for a replacement. If the class was dropped because of weak enrollment, you will need to prove that you will make every effort to bring those figures up.

If you plan to market your seminar to corporations, call and ask for the person in charge of training.

Take a hint from all those telemarketers and use a phone script. You don't need to write out every word. But do write out your main selling points just in case you go brain dead as soon as you hear a real voice at the end of the line. See the telephone script in the Examples Section of the Appendix.

Sometimes the sponsoring group will want to interview you in person. Dress professionally. Bring a copy of your presentation description and any other pertinent material. They need speakers who are organized and dependable. Be friendly and enthusiastic about your topic. These people know their customers and what sells, so be willing to compromise. They may want to change your title, your description or the length of time. Offering a menu of different topics and times will give them the impression that you are "easy to work with" and that's a great reputation to have.

Plan to follow up with all these contacts. If they ask for more information, get it to them immediately. It will show them how professional you are, and how eager you are to work with them.

SETTING UP YOUR OWN SEMINAR

One of the best ways to get people to attend your own self-sponsored seminar is to send out invitations to those on your existing database or to rent a mailing list of hot prospects. Perhaps you can even exchange mailing lists with an associate.

Many successful seminar facilitators place ads in newspapers and trade journals.

Your offer should be compelling.

Just remember, your offer should be very compelling. I would recommend that you hire a professional to write your ads and direct mail pieces. These are the people who can make this approach really work for you.

Because you are underwriting all the costs of your seminar, it is wise to develop some sort of preliminary budget just to give you some guidelines. Keeping track of all your expenses for each seminar will also help you evaluate in the future whether this type of promotional cost is really paying off. Check out the Seminar Budget Worksheet on the order form in the back of this book.

Picking the right location for your seminar will be key to its success. If you book a plush cruise ship or an exotic resort, people's curiosity may draw them to you. Many seminars are held in local hotels that provide the meeting room, food and audio-visual equipment—for a fee, of course. Select a place in which your prospective clients will be comfortable. It should be easy to locate. And the parking should be plentiful.

It is best to visit the facility before you sign a contract. Ideally, you can observe a presentation being made in the actual room you would be using. Note the room set-up and the ventilation. Observe whether the speaker is easily seen and heard. Notice your own first impressions of the entire facility. Did you feel welcome? Was the meeting room easy to find? How about the restrooms, phones and restaurant?

It saddens me to add this, but it's also important to consider security issues in making your hotel choice. What looks like a charming neighborhood during the day when you do your inspection may turn into a frightening place at night, which may turn off many of your potential attendees.

If your company does not have established credit with them, many hotels will ask for a deposit at the time you sign the contract. Be sure to include a cancellation clause in the contract just in case your seminar does not get the preregistration results you are hoping for.

Often your contract will note the room set-up you need. Peek ahead to Chapter 9 for the advantages of each of your various choices. You'll also want to order a long registration table and a couple of chairs to be set up either just outside or inside the meeting room's main door.

Remember, everything is negotiable. In the hotel business there are set prices and then there are the prices that are finally agreed upon. Once you have chosen your meeting room, you can also bargain on the prices on the beverages, and food service and audio-visual equipment.

It's going to be worth your while to carefully communicate all your expectations to the facility's management right up to the moment you finish your seminar. If you do not get what you requested, it will sabotage your success. Double-check *everything*. Do not assume things will be there just because they are in your contract. Your clients are worth this extra effort. And you will make a smoother presentation knowing the details are being taken care of.

CUSTOMIZE YOUR TALK

People feel honored if you take the time to really understand their needs and concerns. You can customize your presentation by asking the meeting planner for a list of questions the group would like answered. Then address those issues in your talk.

> ***People feel honored when you take the time to understand their needs and concerns.***

Another smart thing to do is to read a year's worth of that group's newsletters. This will give you a sense of their current issues and the leaders of the group. Also, give some thought to interviewing the leaders and finding out how you can be of service to them.

BOOKING THOSE DATES

If your goal is to present one or two of these talks a month (and, believe me, that should keep you rolling in clients and referrals!) you need to be well organized. One of the worst things you could do is to forget your commitment and be a no-show. Using the Intake Form in the "Worksheets for Giving Speeches and Seminars" packet will help you tremendously. (See the order form at the back of this book.) On this one form you have all the information you need to cover when booking your gigs.

Pick a date that is going to work for you as well as them. Many times there isn't much choice. It's their standard meeting day and they need a speaker. Just be sure that you allow yourself enough time to prepare so you can do a terrific job. If it's up to you to determine the date, be sure to avoid competing community events such as holidays, fairs and sporting events. When working with a program planner, let them advise you as to what days of the week and times of day work best.

Ask about the timelines and agenda for the event. It's important to know exactly where you fit in. For instance, will you be speaking after everyone has just forked down a gigantic lunch? Good to know, because you'll need to jazz up your presentation with humor, stories and maybe even some audience participation just to keep people from nodding off.

Of course, if you have taken the time to visit this group beforehand, many of these questions will be answered for you. Be clear on how the room will be set up and what type of

The more you know about your audience, the more you can customize your presentation so they feel you truly understand them.

microphone you'll be using, if any. Discuss the visual aids that you need and what they have available. Find out if there will be time for and if they prefer a question-and-answer session.

Probably your most important discussion at the time of the booking will be regarding the audience. The more you know about them the more you can customize your presentation so they feel you truly understand them. First ask how many folks there will be. You'll need that number for handouts. Find out their age, sex, professions, where they live, current concerns, special interests, etc. Do all that you can to weave this information into your talk.

If you get a chance, here's a fantastic question to ask because you'll usually get just a ton of information that will contribute to your speaking success. Ask who their last speaker was, what they spoke about and how the group liked them. If they tell you something like he was really funny but we didn't get much out of it, you'll know to ease up on the humor and really pack in the value. If they remark that the previous speaker was very knowledgeable but the audience didn't like her much, try to find out why. And know that you will need to use more techniques to connect with this audience, such as self-deprecating humor and personal stories.

DEALING WITH PAYMENTS

Have you ever heard people talk about working the "rubber-chicken circuit"? That phrase is used to describe the type of meals often served at meetings where you may be the guest speaker. And usually the meal, which hopefully tastes better than rubber chicken, is all the payment you receive. (Most of us are so nervous before we speak we don't think of eating the meal even if it does look good!)

At times, you may be offered some sort of honorarium, which is nice since it helps to cover your costs. Later on, should you decide to make money speaking, negotiating the speaking fee is a big deal. But for now, if your only goal is to attract more clients and referrals, then let the meeting planner bring up money. Here's a dynamite marketing idea—how about asking to be compensated by getting a copy of their membership list instead of any money. Won't that be much more valuable to you?

Different adult education institutions pay in different ways. Some schools pay on an hourly basis. Other organizations offer a fee split where you are paid a percentage, anywhere from 20 to 60% of the gross revenue. Still others will pay you a base amount. Don't be surprised if some schools want you to sign a contract. Actually it's not a bad idea to have something that spells out who is responsible for what. You do not want to be surprised by a whopping bill for room rental or an overhead projector. On the other hand, some schools may even take on the cost of copying your handouts.

If you are speaking at a convention, ask to have your literature inserted in the meeting packet that goes to each participant. That will benefit you far more than any cash payment.

Before we leave this subject we need to tip-toe over some very sensitive ground. If you are sponsoring your own seminar, take a giant step out of this paragraph—the subject does not apply to you. What we are discussing here is the importance of determining how this group feels about you promoting your service and products. Many groups have been severely burned by superaggressive salespeople who have spent the entire time hawking their wares. There are even some community colleges that absolutely forbid offering any products for sale to their enrollees. So tread lightly here. It's very useful if you can observe another speaker addressing this group, so you can see what's acceptable. One way to gently approach this subject is to ask if you could have a table set up at the back of the room for your brochures and other information of interest to the audience.

When a person does not respond to your letter or phone call, do not assume that they do not want you.

A final word, about which many of you who have been in business for a while already know. The word is "persistence." You'll need it in going after your booking goals. When a person does not respond to your letter or phone call, do not assume that they do not want you. Assume that they, like most of us, are swamped. This is especially true for volunteers who coordinate the meetings for a favorite group. Keep at it. Your persistence will pay off.

7

ATTRACTING THE BEST PROSPECTS TO YOUR PRESENTATIONS

Now that you've booked your speaking gigs, it's time to fill your audiences with tons of ripe prospects. Don't leave this promotional work up to the meeting planner. The more you are involved the better results you'll experience. This chapter includes not only the various tools you will need to market your presentations, but also numerous successful ways to market your event.

PREPARE YOUR MARKETING TOOL KIT

Although you may not use all of these tools for every one of your presentations, it is wise to have them ready to go the moment you do need them.

◆ PREPARE YOUR ONE-MINUTE COMMERCIAL

When I first started my own business, a marketing friend of mine suggested that I create a "one-minute commercial" for myself. I thought it was a bit silly but I did it anyway and have never regretted it.

What's the first thing people ask you after you have been introduced? "So what do you do?" If you prepare a short commercial that mentions your presentation, you can easily sail into your answer. You may even sway them to attend or send a friend. Remember to include the benefits people will get from coming to hear you.

◆ Create Short Articles on Your Topic

The subject matter can be a spin-off of something you are including in your presentation. Write one or two basic articles, usually around 500 to 1,000 words. And then tailor it for a particular audience. Once you've got some solid articles, you can use them over and over again.

Find articles you like in your target publication and imitate them. (Don't copy them, but follow their general structure.) Be sure to pick publications your target audience is reading.

Remember, you are an expert on this topic, so write like an authority. But also let your sense of humor and personality shine through so that you sound approachable. Share your examples and stories freely, as they will make the article a pleasure to read.

◆ Write Up a News Release

Ever read a news article about someone speaking to a particular group? Guess what? It was the someone—the speaker—who probably wrote the news article! Often the organization that sponsors your presentation will do this, but be sure to ask. If they don't, make sure you do. This is just another way to present yourself to the public as an expert. It's possible that a potential client will contact you after reading about you in the paper or hearing about you on radio or TV.

The information about your presentation may be listed in a calendar of events section of the paper or a public service announcement on radio and TV. These are very short and give only the bare facts.

In order to get more exposure, you need to include a hook. Something which is newsworthy. Something which will make people take notice. If your topic is controversial or based on new information it will be much more interesting.

Composing your own news releases can be a bit intimidating at first, but you'll soon see there is a basic formula and all you need do is drop in the details. Refer to the Appendix for a sample news release and further resources for how to write them.

◆ PREPARE A FLYER

In the last chapter, we prepared a flyer that included the title of our presentation and its description plus some information about why we are qualified to speak on this topic. We used it to sell our program to the meeting planner. Now let's take that same flyer and add the where, when and for whom. You may also wish to spice this up with some attractive graphics and color. See the Examples Section of the Appendix.

For those of you planning to self-sponsor a seminar through direct response marketing—mail, e-mail, etc.—you'll want to create a compelling sales letter to use with your flyer. Or you may choose to create an extensive brochure that covers all the information in one unit.

◆ HAVE A PUBLICITY PHOTO TAKEN

The photo of yourself that you share with your meeting planner and the media must be high-quality. Remember, you are creating an image of someone who is competent and professional. That charming vacation shot of you taken by a family member just doesn't work. Nor will a glamour shot. We don't want people confused when they see the real you.

Black and white photos work best. And a 5×7" or 8×10" is just fine. Have several copies made, as you don't always get them back. Be sure to put your name on the back with a sticker or soft-tipped pen.

Head shots are great, although action shots of you making a presentation are also useful. If your computer has the capability, you may want to scan these so you can print them on demand. Be sure you get your photographer's permission to make copies.

◆ PREPARE A PRESS KIT

A press kit is a folder with pockets that contain many of the items we have listed above. The media is accustomed to receiving press kits. But you will also need it if you plan to have corporations sponsor your presentations. A nice-looking press kit will be a necessity if you decide to start charging fees for your speeches and seminars. Lots more on that in Chapter 15.

You can find a nice assortment of these folders in office supply stores. Select the kind that have pockets on either side when you open it up. Pick a conservative color that blends in well with your business cards and stationery. Look for matching envelopes.

After you have given several presentations, you might wish to record your speech or seminar and include it in your press kit.

◆ GATHER TESTIMONIALS

> ***A satisfied customer is one of your best selling tools.***

A satisfied customer is one of your best selling tools. Use what people have said about your presentations to persuade a meeting planner to book you or to persuade someone to attend your next speech or seminar.

Asking for a letter of recommendation after your presentation is a super way to get "paid." If you've done an outstanding job, most meeting planners are more than willing to put their glowing remarks down on paper—although sometimes it takes a little nudging on your part to get the task completed.

If you use a participant feedback form, leave a space for your participants to comment on your presentation and ask for permission to quote them. See the example feedback form in the Appendix.

Keep an ongoing file of these testimonials. They can be very valuable to you. And you'll find yourself using them time and time again.

◆ KEEP A "SWIPE FILE"

As you begin to start thinking about how you will market your presentations, start a file of other people's printed material that you really like. This is often call a "swipe file." You'll be surprised how often you will refer to it when you are designing your own material. Also, use this file to save any creative ideas you get for promoting your speeches and seminars.

◆ SET UP A WORKABLE BUDGET

You will probably spend more money promoting your talks at the beginning, until you discover which methods work best. A budget will help keep your spending in line. Find a formula that works best for you. Many professionals use a percentage, say 10%, of gross revenue. That revenue figure is calculated by taking the target goal for the number of clients acquired times your average client sales figure.

Now that you have prepared your marketing tool kit. Let's examine ways to put each of these tools to good use.

Being known in the community as a speaker will not only help you attract people who want to hear you, it will help you hear about other speaking opportunities.

20 WAYS TO MARKET YOURSELF AND YOUR PRESENTATION

Writing up a marketing plan for each of your presentations will be very beneficial. Pick the following techniques that will work best for you and place them on a timeline. Then estimate the costs of each task. Now you have a workable plan that you can use over and over again.

1. OFFER TO WRITE ARTICLES

As soon as a meeting planner confirms a speaking date with you, offer to submit an article for their newsletter. Most organizations are thirsty for articles and will more than welcome this offer. Who knows, it may turn into a regular column! If they don't have a newsletter, find a magazine, newspaper or journal that members of the audience do read.

If the article is scheduled to come out before you speak to the group, include just enough to make them see that you know what you are talking about and that they could learn more by coming to hear you. If the article comes out after your presentation, reinforce the items you covered and make it clear how they contact you. That's also a nice way to reach out to those who missed your presentation. Better yet, offer to write two articles, one before and one after.

2. NETWORK

Getting yourself known in the community as a speaker can be very beneficial. Not only will you attract people who want to hear you, you will also hear about other speaking opportunities.

This is not a time to be pushy, forceful, flip or shy. Simply bring your topic up in conversation and mention some of the benefits of attending. This is when you can use your one-minute commercial. Of course, always carry your flyer with you so you can give them all the details when they ask.

Think carefully about where your target population hangs out and go there. Let me give you an example. Let's say your talk is especially targeted for working women. You should make every effort to attend networking breakfasts and professional women's meetings. Sometimes they are looking for a luncheon speaker. Other times they are planning conferences. You would be doing them a big favor by offering to make a presentation and furthering their knowledge of your subject matter and you.

Don't forget to ask for referrals. People usually want to help and you never know who they know. They may give you leads for sponsors and they may tell you where to find attendees. But you'll never know unless you ask. It is also imperative that you follow up on every lead given to you. If you don't, people will stop offering them.

Take this referral idea one step further and ask your audience and your satisfied customers to tell others about your upcoming presentations. Some will even be willing to hand out flyers for you.

3. GET YOUR FLYER UP ON BULLETIN BOARDS

Distribute your flyer all around the neighborhood and on virtual bulletin boards — wherever you think your target clients might see it. Look around your neighborhood. There are bulletin boards in grocery stores, community centers, churches and libraries. Use brightly colored paper to attract attention. Be sure you include all the details, like place, time and date. You might use a flyer that has tear-off strips at the bottom to make it easy for the reader to take home the contact information.

Some seminar leaders have even made up attractive full-color posters to promote their events in the community.

4. USE YOUR VOICE MAIL TO PROMOTE

Give some thought to the message you are leaving for your callers to hear. Mentioning that you are unavailable because you are teaching a class is an excellent way to promote yourself.

On your phone message you could also offer to send a flyer to any caller who wants more information.

Yes, meeting planners do talk to one another. It would be wonderful to gain a reputation as someone who gets back to them quickly. Because of deadline pressures, some continuing education staff may need to hear from you almost immediately. Make it a point to return your calls as soon as possible.

5. INCLUDE THE TITLE OF YOUR TALK IN YOUR BROCHURE

Next time you print up the brochure for your business include the fact that you make presentations and their titles. This is an excellent way to establish yourself as an expert in your field.

6. ADD "SPEAKER" TO YOUR JOB TITLE ON YOUR BUSINESS CARD

7. MENTION YOUR PRESENTATIONS IN YOUR NEWSLETTER

If you have your own newsletter, be sure to list all your speaking gigs in there. Even if your readers cannot attend, they will know that you make presentations, and they might invite you to speak to their group. Also, this strengthens their belief that you really know what you are talking about.

If you send your clients a newsletter or any literature prepared by someone else, consider inserting a flyer with information about your upcoming speeches and seminars.

8. GIVE PERSONAL INVITATIONS (TICKETS) TO YOUR PROSPECTS

A personal invitation or a ticket is a wonderful way to make someone feel special. It also shows that the content of your presentation was customized for them and therefore they will get a great deal of value from attending. An RSVP creates an urgency that they need to commit to coming so that they are guaranteed a seat and that you are preparing material just for them.

Mail these out to folks on your mailing list. And distribute them to people you meet while networking.

Still another idea is to give these tickets to your current clients and ask them to pass them on to their friends. If they are satisfied with the work you have done for them, they will be more than willing to share you with their friends and associates.

9. CREATE TICKLERS (TIP SHEETS, ETC.) AND GIVE TO ONE AND ALL

A one-page tip sheet is very easy to produce and something you can use over and over to promote your talks. An accountant could create a list of the ten most common mistakes people make on their tax returns. A career counselor could create a humorous list of creative answers to job interview questions.

These ticklers can be in the form of 8½ × 11" pages, bookmarks, three-panel brochures or whatever. Of course, somewhere on the form will be information about you and your upcoming presentations.

These work so well in giving folks a feel for what you are like and what you know. They are also an excellent item to include in your press kit and in any articles that you write.

10. PERSONALLY ASK CENTERS OF INFLUENCE TO ATTEND

Many people who could become a fountain of referrals for you may be reluctant to share your name until they hear you speak. Invite them to attend your presentation as a guest. Then follow up with a thank-you phone call or note afterwards.

If they happen to be experienced presenters and you feel comfortable asking their advice, see if they have any suggestions for ways to make your presentation even stronger.

> ***People who could become fountains of referrals may be reluctant to share your name until they've heard you speak.***

Tell them how much you would appreciate referrals from them. And let them know you are available if you can assist them in any way.

11. DIRECT MAIL CAMPAIGN

Your success in conducting a direct mail campaign will depend on two key factors: renting a terrific list of names and designing a terrific sales brochure. Working with experts will pay off royally for you. You'll also want to set up a solid budget and a realistic timeline. Refer to the Appendix for some great direct mail resources.

If your seminar is sponsored by an educational institution, offer to provide your mailing list to them so they can use it when they send out their catalogs.

12. PHONE CAMPAIGN

"Cold-calling" a rented list of strangers and asking them to attend your presentation may have rather limited results. But conducting a phone campaign as one element of a total marketing campaign may prove to be very effective.

For instance, if you meet someone at a networking event who expresses some interest in your topic, call them up and personally invite them to attend. Or if someone mentioned after your speech that her group uses speakers, give her a call and see if she can work you in.

Another phone technique that works extremely well is to call those who have registered for your seminar the day before and remind them. You may even end up giving them extra information about driving directions or parking. This really shows them how much you want them to attend. And that you are willing to go the extra mile to be of service to them.

13. DISTRIBUTE NEWS RELEASES

A standard news release should be part of your tool kit. Target the publications and electronic media that are appropriate—in other words, the ones that reach your target audience. Be sure you have made it newsworthy so that they run it.

Be sure to send out your news release in plenty of time. Ask the publications when their deadlines are. Sometimes they need as much as a month's notice.

Should a newspaper decide to do a feature story on you, ask them to mention the fact that you are giving a talk and how the readers can contact you or the sponsor for more information.

14. GET QUOTED

I realize that this may be a real stretch for some of you, but I think you will find that getting quoted in the media is really fairly easy. Reporters always need experts to quote. And really you are just sharing the type of information you give your clients every day. They will appreciate the fact that you are readily available by phone as they are always working under tight deadlines. Give them captivating examples and attention-grabbing phrases.

One of the best ways to become established as an expert is to respond to a news article or report. Simply call the source, offer your expert information on what was presented and mention that you are available in the future if they need that type of information. This would be a terrific time to refer to your upcoming presentation, as it will help to establish you as an expert on the subject.

15. PLACE ADS

Putting ads in newspapers and magazines can be expensive but worthwhile if you do it carefully. First of all, be sure that your target audience reads that particular publication.

Newspaper ads are effective for free introductory seminars. And teaser ads work well to get people interested in your topic and call for more information.

Start clipping other people's ads for seminars. Examine them. Does the headline draw? Do they use benefit-focused copy? Was it well placed in the paper?

Test out your own ads. Keep revising them until you find one that keeps on working.

16. RADIO AND TV

If you sent a news release to your local radio and television stations and you are speaking to a nonprofit group, your talk will probably be mentioned in a public service announcement. Stations are required by law to make these, but it could be that they are aired in the wee hours of the morning. Anyway, it is still worth a try.

But also target a particular show or personality and send your entire press kit to them. It is imperative that you are clear on ways your information would be of interest to their listeners.

If you are asked to be on an interview show it's best to provide your own sample question list. This takes the interviewer off the hook to think up questions, plus you will be well prepared to answer them.

17. MENTION YOUR OTHER PRESENTATIONS

So you are giving a speech to the local chamber and you have a self-sponsored seminar coming up in two weeks. Mention it. Invite them to come. Tell them they will get even more valuable information because you will have more time. If you have done a good job presenting, people will appreciate finding out how they can get more of you. Of course, don't overdo it. Weave it into your speech and handout material.

18. MENTION OTHER TITLES IN INTRO AND/OR PRESENTATION

Provide a dynamic introduction that explains why you are qualified to speak on this subject, mentions your other accomplishments, refers to your other presentations, emphasizes what they are about to learn and reassures them of its benefits. The introduction should also make your audience eager to hear you. (An example is included in the Appendix.)

19. ASK THE PREVIOUS SPEAKER TO MENTION YOU

This is a very effective technique to use during a conference or convention where there will be a speaker line-up. If the previous speaker refers to you (in a positive way, of course), it will build anticipation and excitement about hearing you. People may even decide to attend your workshop instead of another.

Be sure to do this for the speaker following you.

If you've done a good job presenting, people will want to know how they can get more of you.

20. MAKE IT KNOWN THAT YOU ARE DONATING YOUR FEE TO CHARITY

This is an outstanding way for you show that you are willing to do something extra for your community. Believe me, people want to do business with people like that.

On your seminar flyer, note that all or part of the registration fees, even a token amount of $5, will be donated to such-and-such charity. Now your attendees have an opportunity to support their favorite charity while coming to hear you.

If you are given an honorarium for your speech, announce that you will be donating the money to a favorite cause of that group. Take it a bit further and make it a contest. Tell them you will donate a dollar for everyone who gives you their business card after your speech.

One more idea on this notion is to make your speech or seminar part of a nonprofit fundraiser. Let's say you are a financial whiz and you talk about how to finance your child's college education as part of an annual fundraiser for parents' group. Getting involved in arrangements like this is a terrific win for everybody.

8

TECHNIQUES FOR PROMOTING YOUR SERVICES/PRODUCTS DURING THE PRESENTATION

Making your sales pitch during your presentation can be very tricky. If you go overboard and sell too much, you will turn your audience off. On the other hand, if you give a soft sell or no sell at all, you have wasted a golden opportunity to attract more clients. This chapter will help you find a rewarding balance between the two extremes. It also provides you with lots of techniques for promoting from the platform.

Our main purpose in presenting speeches and seminars is to let our prospects get a taste of what we are like. They are buying our expertise, but more than that they want someone they can trust. Someone they respect and can put their confidence in. Someone who really cares about them. People who give you referrals must feel you possess the 3 C's—confidence, competence and compassion.

> ***One of the best ways to show that you care and will work hard for people is to present a great talk that relates to their needs.***

GIVE AN EXCELLENT CLIENT-CENTERED TALK

One of the best ways to show that you care and will work hard for people is to present a great talk. One that relates to their needs. In the previous chapters we looked at what needs to be in the content of such talks. Remember, you don't want to sound like a giant infomercial. You must give value! And the upcoming chapters on delivery will give you tips on how to be most effective. But probably the most important thing that you can do during your talk is to just be you.

Be real. If you enjoy telling jokes, tell one. If you like talking about your family, say so. If you are proud of what you have been able to do for some of your clients, talk about that. Don't feel you need to be like anyone else. And thank goodness we don't need to be perfect. By being real, by showing people what you are passionate about, people will connect with you. And don't we all prefer to work with people we like?

ESTABLISH CREDIBILITY

Of course, besides being likeable we also need to establish our credibility. Your audience wants to be sure that you know what you are talking about. Here are three techniques that will help you establish yourself as an authority.

First, name-drop your important clients. Unless there is an issue of confidentiality, mention the people and companies you have worked with. If your clients are well known in your community, others will want to jump on the bandwagon.

Second, showcase your work. If you're an architect or designer, why not a slide show of your portfolio, so people can see what you do. For the rest of us, think very methodically about sharing one of your client's success stories during your presentation. The subtle message will be, "if you hire me I can get similar results for you."

Third, present yourself as an authority figure. Dress like one. Walk and sit like one. And talk like one. Like it or not, we are a very image-focused society. People want to believe in you. Don't give them any excuse not to.

FOSTER TRUST

People seem to be very skeptical today. Many have been burned before. There seems to be a natural resistance to anyone pitching their stuff. Sometimes this reveals itself as a reluctance to deal with any of the concerns you are addressing. There are a couple things you can do to lower this resistance.

First, check out your own commitment level. Do you passionately believe that the services and products you are offering will make a significant, positive change in these people's lives? If not, it won't work. Most people sense when they are being conned. Get excited about what you are doing and the positive impact that has on others.

Get excited about what you are doing and the positive impact that it has on others.

Second, make yourself approachable. One the best ways to do this is through self-deprecating humor and personal stories. We'll discuss this thoroughly in upcoming chapters.

Third, do nothing which is out of integrity. Remember that your audience is constantly checking you out. If you do anything which undermines your honesty, they'll back away from you. Let me give you an example. This can be very subtle stuff. I once heard an investment counselor give a speech where he was trying to persuade the audience to trust him with several thousands of dollars of their money. Throughout the presentation he used someone else's copyrighted material. Yes, I know it's done. Often. But think about the message he was relaying. I've also seen the trust factor blown to smithereens when a presenter tells an inappropriate joke. Even if people laugh, there is an underlying current of doubt about what other inappropriate things this person does. And how much this person respects their own clients.

Just remember, you're trying to establish trust, so do everything you can to present yourself as worthy of that trust.

SEVEN THINGS YOU CAN DO TO ASK FOR THEIR BUSINESS

1. INSERT A "COMMERCIAL" IN YOUR INTRODUCTION

If someone else is going to introduce you, let them promote you. Ask them to use an introduction written by you that includes a description of the services and products you provide. If you are making some sort of free offer, let your introducer share the news and you'll start off your talk with a very friendly audience.

2. USE THOSE HANDOUTS

Be sure that everything you give out to your audience has information on how to get in touch with you. This includes your handouts, brochures and business cards. Each participant should walk away with at least one document that describes your services.

One clever thing to do is to develop a short "quiz" that will demonstrate their need for your services. For example, a counselor could distribute a stress quiz which demonstrates the need for more copying strategies. Offer to collect and "grade" them. This gives you a perfect reason to contact them further.

3. COLLECT THEIR NAMES AND ADDRESSES

If you have done a good job in selecting your target audience, collecting their names and addresses is like mining for gold. This will be your means of making them your clients. Finding out who they are is the first step of your follow-up marketing plan where you arrange to contact them by phone, mail or electronically.

One of the best ways to get this information is to offer a prize or several prizes to some lucky candidates. Of course, you will need to collect everyone's business card in order to make the drawing. People love the possibility of winning something, so most will eagerly toss their card in the hat. Of course, after the drawing is done, you've got a database to work with.

4. SOLICIT FEEDBACK AND SO MUCH MORE

Here is what you may want to include on your feedback form:

- Evaluate your presentation.
- Ask for suggestions about future topics.
- Cement their learning. Do this by asking people to summarize the most important thing they learned. And with their permission you can use these later for endorsements.
- And (this is extremely important) get their name and address. This is so important to some presenters that they do it first, so they do not miss anyone in the rush to leave at the end.

Devise a means of collecting *all* feedback forms as people leave the room. Some presenters give a prize for completion. Others hold a drawing of the forms and present a gift to the winner.

My favorite feedback form is in the Examples Section of the Appendix. Feel free to adapt it for your own use.

Your goal is to keep some sort of connection with people after they walk out the door.

5. OFFER A CONNECTING NEXT STEP

Your goal here is to keep some sort of connection with people after they walk out the door. You might think about offering a free half-hour phone or in-person consultation to get them to start working with you. Or offer to send them some special material that relates to their needs. If you have a newsletter, offer to send them your next issue.

Coupons also work well here. You could offer a reduced fee or free time slot on your first meeting.

Get creative with what you can offer to continue your connection. Build in some sort of urgency for people to take action today. It's very easy to put something like this off, so offer a special bonus that is valid for a specific, brief period of time.

6. GIVE OUT PROMOTIONAL ITEMS

There are endless ways to foster name recognition and get your message out. Here are a few ideas: bookmarks, tip sheets, laminated cards, badges, posters, etc. An accountant friend of mine distributes a handy ruler. It includes his name, phone number and a reminder that he is a small business tax expert.

Take a glance at the pens on your desk. You probably have one with a logo and business name on it. Pens, notepads, key-rings, refrigerator magnets and hundreds of other ad specialties are gimmicks to cultivate name recognition. These goodwill trinkets are worth trying. Then evaluate to see if they are worth the money for you. Suppliers can be found under Stationery—Wholesale & Retail and Awards/Novelties in your Yellow Pages.

7. ASK FOR REFERRALS, ASK FOR THEIR BUSINESS

> ***Simply state how much you enjoyed being with them and that you would very much enjoy being of service to them.***

This suggestion may seem obvious, but so often we simply forget to ask for what we want. This can work in well at the conclusion of your presentation. Simply state how much you enjoyed being with them and that you would very much enjoy being of service to them. If you have convinced them of the value of your services and they like you, you'll be like a magnet for new clients and great referrals.

TIMING YOUR PITCH

Usually the best time to make your sales pitch is during the last few minutes of your speech. This is after you have given them something of value and persuaded them that they need your services. Make it clear that you want their business and exactly what you are offering them.

If you are presenting a seminar, you may wish to time your pitch just before the first break. That way people will have plenty of time to talk with you either during the break or after of the seminar.

Still another technique is to schmooze with people during the meal. People are usually relaxed while they are eating, and more approachable. Of course, don't monopolize their time—let them get back to that yummy chicken.

TALKING AFTERWARDS

Don't think you can rest after you have finished your presentation. In fact, just after you give your talk may be when you do your most work. Often people want to talk to you on a one-to-one basis. Think carefully about where you want to physically locate yourself. If you have set up a display at the back of the room, quickly move to it as soon as you are done speaking.

Be prepared to make appointments with people if they are eager to work with you.

Think about what you want to say if people want to discuss your fees right then and there.

9

HOW TO BEST PREPARE FOR YOUR PRESENTATION

Besides making your former Scout leader very proud, being well prepared has two major payoffs. First of all, it will give your audience the strong impression that you are a thoughtful and thorough professional. The message is that if you put that much effort into a free presentation you'll do the same, and more, for the clients you serve. Spending time preparing for your presentation will also decrease your nervousness dramatically. You will have practiced well, maximized the facilities to enhance your performance and prevented many of those nerve-racking, last-minute emergencies.

MAKE USEFUL NOTES FOR YOURSELF

The length and look of one's notes are unique to each and every speaker. Try different techniques until you find what works best for you. Most speakers use an outline or key phrases from their presentation. Don't plan to read your speech. It will instantly put your audience to sleep.

Here are some helpful hints:

- Be sure to number each page or index card, just in case you should drop them.
- Select a large type (20-pt.), so you can read your notes from a distance. This is especially important if you usually wear glasses and won't have them on while you speak.

- Make the lettering and symbols dark so you can read them in dim lighting.
- Use underlining and asterisks to emphasize points you wish to stress.
- Use stickers or draw symbols to cue yourself at significant moments. You can use lips to remind yourself to pause and take a breath a smiley face to prompt a grin and a light bulb to remind yourself that it's time to turn off the overhead projector.
- Determine how long each section of your presentation will take and jot down what time it should be when you come to that section. If your notes say 8:30 and your watch says 8:40, you need to speed up and drop out some extra items.
- Use colorful highlighter pens to remind yourself to emphasize certain points.
- Always carry your notes with you when traveling to your presentation. Don't risk losing them by shipping them or checking them through luggage claim.

WRITE YOUR OWN INTRODUCTION

You won't always have someone to introduce you, but if you do, it's nice to provide them with some information about you. There is no guarantee that they will use it, but if they do, it will help to warm up your audience. It's a wise practice to make two copies—mail one in advance, and bring the other copy with you on the day of your presentation, just in case.

Introductions usually run about 100 to 150 words. Be sure to double-space your material and use a large font so it is easy to read. Ask your introducer to present it word for word so that they get it just the way you want it.

A bad introduction can taint your audience's image of you and undermine your credibility and confidence. Don't let this happen. Provide a strong written introduction that explains why you are qualified to speak on this subject, mentions your other accomplishments, emphasizes what they are about to learn and reassures them of the benefits of the information. It should also make your audience eager to hear you. (There's an example in the Appendix.)

MAXIMIZE THE ROOM SET-UP

Your room set-up can greatly affect your message. Many times you do not have much control over the situation. You are the invited guest and they have been using the same set-up for years. Other times your event planner will ask you what kind of set-up you prefer. Some professionals hold seminars in their own office complex. The advantages of this are that you are in control of the set-up and can easily run to your office for anything you might need.

> ***Your room set-up can greatly affect your message.***

It is always wise to determine the room arrangement at the time you book your gig. Be sure to make note of it on your intake sheet. Here are some basic options:

- *Banquet Style* – Circular tables throughout the room with 6 to 12 people sitting around each table. You will probably be speaking from a long, elevated "head table" which may have a podium. You can pretty much predict that this will be the set-up if a meal is served. Because of the circular arrangement about one-third of the audience will have their backs to the head table. If they seem to be somewhat shy about moving their chairs around before you speak, you might take a moment at the beginning of your speech and invite them to do so. Or ask your introducer to do this. It is important that everyone is comfortable and can see you.

If you have a portable microphone and you are feeling brave, it's nice to free yourself of the formality of the head table and move out into the audience while you speak. Just be wary of steps, cords and a myriad of things that can end up in your pathway.

Also, be prepared to speak over the clatter of dishes being cleared by the wait staff. What is nice about this room set-up is that the people at each table have become acquainted and are a natural small discussion group.

- *Theater Style* – Just like going to the movies: everyone on a chair facing forward; sometimes includes a center aisle. Terrific for large groups and for presenting lecture style; awkward if your audience needs to take a lot of notes since they must use their laps.

Note: If you get a chance to present in an amphitheater, audience members will probably have a small surface to write on and they will be able to see you easily. Just remember that this is a theater and you need to make everything BIG—your movements, your voice (unless you are using a microphone) and your visual aids, especially if you are writing on a board or flip chart.

If you wish to encourage your audience to interact while sitting in theater style, ask them to introduce themselves to their neighbor or give them small group tasks.

- *Classroom Style* – Students sit at tables facing forward, just like first grade. This is better for participants who need to write notes but sometimes the folks in the back get lost. Also it feels a lot like being back in grade school. You can move up and down the center aisle in order to get closer. Participants mostly get to see you and the backs of the people in front of them. It really inhibits discussion since participants can't look at each other without doing some major body contortions.

Here's an adaptation of this basic set-up that really contributes to group participation: angle each table in a herringbone pattern. In other words, place the end to the table nearest the center aisle back a foot or two. Do this for each table on both sides of the aisle. In this way, participants in the same row but on opposite sides of the aisle can see each other and talk freely. You will be amazed what a difference this one change makes in the amount of interaction.

- *U-Shaped with Tables* – This is my favorite for groups smaller than 30. Nobody is stuck in the back and everyone can see each other. It encourages more group interaction. And it gives me more room to move.

An adaptation of this is the giant boardroom or conference table where everyone sits around in usually very plush chairs.

MAKE ARRANGEMENTS

Get there early. Realize that you will not always (in fact, you will rarely) have an ideal room set-up. Be prepared to move furniture, if it's appropriate. It's not a pleasant task, although it is one good way to work off extra adrenaline – just don't get too sweaty! Often, participants who arrive early are more than happy to lend you a hand. It is worth the extra effort and it shows the participants that you really care about their comfort and success.

I once gave a workshop in a hotel room with two huge pillars dead center in the room. No matter where I stood, half of my audience could not see me! I certainly paced a lot during that workshop! I recommend that you acknowledge the problem to the audience and state that you will try to do your best for them. However, never complain about it or make any negative remarks about the program planner or the sponsoring organization. You may be angry or disappointed, but don't get the audience involved. It may backfire on you.

SET UP EXTRA TABLES

If you are handling the registration or sign-in, it may help to have an extra table right outside the room entrance or at the back of the room. This is an excellent place to distribute the name tags or tents and your handouts.

If you plan to display items or offer free material, set up a table at the side or back of the room.

Also, be sure you have enough surface space at the front of the room to handle all the materials you will be using throughout the presentation.

HANDOUTS: DON'T LEAVE HOME WITHOUT THEM

In fact, there isn't much point in making a presentation without giving out a handout. This is one of your prime marketing tools. People expect them. They will take them home or back to the office, pass them on to friends, put them on their refrigerator and refer to them years later. Of course your name and all your contact information will be on each and every page.

Be sure that every handout you share has real educational value and is not just sales hype. It shows you care about your audience and truly want to be of service to them. You may also find that when you make your handout informative and comprehensive, it will allow you some flexibility in your presentation to change the time you spend on each point. If you have to skim over some topics in order to cover others, you'll know that everything is thoroughly included in the handout. It's also very wise to attach copies of articles you have written or that have been written about you. This is a nice way to share more useful information and to establish your credibility.

There isn't much point in making a presentation without providing handouts.

It's wise to always bring extras, and encourage people to take additional copies for their friends and business associates. If it is something that will make a clean copy, bring the original along so that someone can make more in a pinch.

For a 20- to 30-minute speech, a one-page, double-sided handout is just fine. You can produce a mini-booklet by folding an 8½ × 11" sheet in half. Usually your handout is a summary of your basic points. Often you can go into more detail on paper than you have time for in your speech. Sometimes you may want to include definitions of terms.

Your one- to two-hour seminars demand much more extensive handouts. Many facilitators create workbooks where the participant has lots of room for personal notations. Some use a format that allows the student to fill in the blanks. Some people create short quizzes or self-evaluation forms. You might also want to include a bibliography and resources for finding further information on your subject. These handouts can be anywhere from five to 20 pages.

Here are numerous ways you can assemble your workbooks: stapled in the upper left-hand corner, stapled all along the side, spiral plastic comb-bound, or inserted into an attractive report folder or three-ring binder. If there aren't too many pages, print them on 11 × 17" sheets, fold in half and staple at the seam. Visit your local copy shop or office supply store and solicit their ideas. Be sure to also ask the costs of your various choices.

By the way, sometimes the group that is sponsoring you is willing to help with the cost of copying. Ask, if you think it would be appropriate. Once in a while an organization will provide a special folder for their members. If so, they may ask you to give them your original in advance, so that they may make copies and stuff them in the folders.

Fancy desktop publishing programs and even most word processing software makes it extremely easy to produce some very attractive handouts. Just remember some basic design concepts or share them with your office staff who are assisting you with this.

- Leave lots of white space.
- Don't be tempted to data-dump. If your page is crammed with information it will not get read, and all your hard work will end up in the recycle bin.
- Use quality paper, and color if possible.
- Good clip art will give it a very professional look.

Once you have developed a good handout to accompany each speech and seminar you offer, make lots of copies and have them ready to go as you leave your office.

For those of you who use handouts produced by someone else, take a few moments to analyze them. Do they really support you and your message? If not, why use them? Sometimes inexperienced professionals feel they need to give their prospects tons of information to convince them of the speaker's value. I hope it is not too much of a shock to learn that most of that paperwork is never read, probably turns the buyer off and it is tossed as quickly as possible. So rethink what you want your audience to remember about you and your service and what really needs to be on your "leave-behind."

Give some thought to what would be the most effective way of distributing your handouts. For short speeches, it's nice to have them on the participants' chairs or tables as they enter the room. You do not want to spend part of your precious speaking time meandering around your audience passing these out. Some presenters distribute the handouts after their speech. They feel that the papers are too distracting and compete for their audience's attention. Still others offer to give everybody a free handout after the speech; and this gives the speaker a chance to meet and speak with folks individually. Others offer handouts (and other gifts, such as pens, notepads, etc.) in exchange for business cards. This is a very effective way to start building your follow-up database, which we will discuss in detail in Chapter 14. Some seminar presenters wait until after a break or until they come to a certain subject before they distribute the handouts. At times, pausing to walk around and distribute material is a nice way to give yourself a breather. Try distributing your material several ways and see which works best for you.

Sometimes people copyright their handouts but I'm not sure why. Sure—when and if you go big time and decide to turn speaking into an additional profit center (see Chapter 15) it makes sense to copyright your stuff and sell it. But quite frankly I would be tickled pink if someone went and made a gazillion copies of my single-page handouts and gave them to everyone they see. Remember, your name and contact information is on every single sheet!

One more note on people's copyrighted material: don't abuse it. This is someone's hard work; don't steal it. It gives a subtle message to your prospects about your value system. It's just not worth it. Create your own masterpieces that you can be proud of. Or obtain written permission from the copyright owner. While we are on the topic of attaining written permission, here's mine to you. As a gift to support your success, you have my permission to make a gazillion copies of the "Worksheets for Giving Speeches and Seminars" which you can order at the back of this book. That's right—they are absolutely copyright-free to you. Using these worksheets each time you make a presentation will keep you focused and assist you in getting the most mileage out of every speaking opportunity.

Of course, one of your most important handouts will be your evaluation form. Refer to that section in Chapter 8.

PRACTICE, PRACTICE, PRACTICE

A well-rehearsed presentation is a lovely gift to yourself and your audience. At times, practicing can be tedious, but the payoffs are well worth it.

There are two levels of practicing—substance and style. The substance of your speech can be practiced while you're driving your car or exercising. Don't memorize it word for word. But you should know the order. And you need to be very familiar with your beginning, conclusion and all of the stories you plan to use. Practicing your presentation style takes a little more effort. It would be ideal if you could practice in a room similar to the one you'll be presenting in. It's also best to rehearse with the visual aids and microphone you will be using. Practice your gestures, try moving to different parts of the stage if possible. Your goal is to make every movement in harmony with the words you are saying. Experiment with different ways to use your voice—volume and speed can add a lot of variety and interest.

> ***A well-rehearsed presentation is a lovely gift to yourself and your audience.***

As you practice, be sure to time your presentation. You may find that you have way too much material and need to whittle it down. Also be certain you allow time for groups exercises, their laughter, and a question-and-answer period, if appropriate.

Of course, one of the absolute best ways to practice is with a video camera or, at least, a tape recorder. Review your tape with a trusted friend or spouse who can give you constructive feedback. Turn the volume down on the video and see if your body language relays the message you intend to give.

Even when you have given the same speech or seminar several times, it never hurts to practice. The audience is always different and worthy of your best effort.

REMINDER PHONE CALLS THE DAY BEFORE

If you self-sponsor your own seminar or have asked special people to be your guests at your presentation, it's good to give them a reminder phone call the day before. Just use the excuse that you wanted to confirm the location with them or be sure they have accurate driving directions. This small gesture will definitely increase your show rate.

If you are working with a meeting planner, it's also smart to place a confirming phone call the day before. This is a terrific time to sew up any loose ends.

THE DAY BEFORE

Start your preparation the day before. You will be doing yourself a favor by assembling as much as you can ahead of time. Our moms were very smart when they laid out all our clothes the night before school. Two minutes before you leave is *not* the best time to remember that the outfit you planned to wear is at the cleaners!

It's also a good idea to pack your notes, the handouts and feedback forms, directions to your destination and, of course, your emergency kit (see Appendix).

Double-check any equipment that you are bringing to be sure it is working properly.

Rehearse your presentation one more time; know that you will give it your best. Focus on the goals you wish to achieve, and then stop worrying.

Although you may be nervous, try to get a good night's sleep and visualize your success.

EAT WELL BEFOREHAND

Eat substantial, healthful meals the day of your program. You'll need it. Some people find that dairy products coat their throat and make it harder to present.

If you are giving an evening program, plan carefully what and when you will eat throughout the day. It's difficult to project your voice over a growling stomach! Many after-dinner speakers choose not to eat the meal provided, but instead eat afterwards.

Eat foods that will give you energy instead of make you lethargic. Fruits are best for this. Avoid caffeine. It will make you more nervous.

PACK FOR THE UNEXPECTED

Murphy's Law (that if something can go wrong, it will) seems to run rampant at the time of any major presentation, so be ready. In the Checklists Section of the Appendix you will find the contents of an emergency kit I have developed over the years. Carry an emergency kit with you always. It will save the day many a time.

PLAN TO ARRIVE EARLY

If you arrive in plenty of time (usually an hour beforehand) you can prevent a lot of hassles. One time I was locked out of a building on a large college campus. It was a Saturday morning, so it was very hard to locate anyone who could help. Finally, a campus police officer showed with not one, but three, fistfuls of keys. It took many agonizing minutes to find the right one, but we still started on time. Whew!

CHECKLISTS ARE YOUR SAFETY NET

Probably one of the most effective things I've done to relieve my own pre-presentation stress is to develop checklists. (Refer to the Appendix. There is one to use before you leave your office and another to review just before you make your presentation.) Customize yours to fit your different topics and visual aids. You'll probably revise them a couple of times. The best time to update them is right after your presentation. Once you've used them, you won't leave home without them—even when you have presented countless times. In that way you'll be positive that everything is covered and you can relax and give it your best.

10

VISUAL AIDS FOR MAXIMUM IMPACT

It is essential that you plan to use at least one visual aid for each of your presentations. They are vital to making your talk memorable.

VISUAL AID EQUIPMENT

Most of us are part of the TV generation and accustomed to watching as we get information. If used correctly, visual aids can greatly enhance your presentation and make your points memorable. Here are some that will do an excellent job for you in getting your material across:

- *Overhead Projector*–A very versatile and powerful aid. Most facilities have one. And you can use it with as few as five people all the way up to several hundred.

Unfortunately, presenters misuse overhead projectors a lot. Yes, I know it is really easy to just go to a copy machine and make a transparency of an interesting article or a business form, but don't do it. It looks very unprofessional and makes it hard for anyone to read. It only frustrates your audience. Instead, include the article or form in your handout. Also, be wary of projecting copyrighted material such as cartoons for all the world to see that you "borrowed" material without permission.

Many beginning speakers tend to overuse transparencies. Don't overload your audience's visual senses. Remember, you are using these to *aid* your presentation, not to make the presentation for you.

Keep the design of your transparencies as simple as possible. Use no more than nine words per page. Select an 18-point font or larger, and pick a font that is plain and easy to read. The bullet format works well. Consider using a few basic colors to jazz up each transparency. And use clip art or cartoon figures to make it more appealing. Of course, software programs like Microsoft's PowerPoint and similar programs make it easy. Orient all your transparencies the same way. Switching back and forth between horizontal and vertical mode is jarring to the viewer.

Be sure to review each transparency on a projector before you actually use it. Walk to the back of the room and see if you can read it easily. Always ask yourself if this transparency is truly helping to make your point. If not, it's not worth using.

Another way to add color and to personalize the items projected is to use specially designed washable pens to circle or underline a particular point. After your show, you can easily wash off the marks with a wet paper towel.

Still another way to use a pen is to place it right on the projector and let it serve as a pointer to the particular item you are discussing.

It may be a smart idea to carry blank transparencies to use on the fly. Should an audience member need further demonstration, you can write out your calculations or draw a simple diagram for everyone to view. Think of it as a portable blackboard. This is a marvelous way to clarify a point or clear up a confusing question. Be ready with a set of colorful overhead projector pens. If the problem comes up in several presentations, make a permanent transparency to cover the situation.

Many presenters like to use transparency frames. They are easier to handle and because they are often pre-punched they are convenient for carrying in a three-ring binder. This makes them very portable and a breeze to store. Frames also help you center the transparency on the projector. This will save you time fiddling to get it right, and again makes you look more professional. But the best reason to use frames is that you can write notes on them and the audience never sees them. It's a neat way to keep yourself on track.

Here's a trick if you want to get fancy. Sometimes you may wish to cover part of the transparency and reveal the information later. Just tape a paper flap over the appropriate areas and simply flip it back when you ready to discuss that topic. Another technique is to place a blank piece of paper on top of the transparency and move it down as you expose more information. It's very effective to put a coin, such as a quarter, on the paper so that the projector's fan does not blow it off. Even then the paper may fall off at the bottom and reveal more than you wanted. Avoid this by leaving the bottom fourth of the transparency blank. Practice using either of these techniques until they are second nature and do not distract you from your presentation.

It is best to practice using an overhead or at least pretending one is there. Often inexperienced speakers (and, sometimes, spacey experienced ones!) walk behind the projector and are temporarily blinded by the bright light. Be sure to stand so that you do not obstruct any participant's view of the screen.

This may sound pretty nitpicky but I am also going to suggest that you practice changing the transparencies as well. Be sure you have one pile for the used transparencies and a different pile for the unviewed ones. It's very easy to mix them up in the heat of a presentation. This can be really unnerving when lots of eyes are bearing down on you, so it's best to develop a system and practice lots.

When you enter the meeting room, decide where you will stand in relation to the projector. This is very important if you plan to use those colorful pens and write on the transparency —unless, of course, you are ambidextrous and can also write facing a bright light. If need be, move the furniture around before the program starts so that you can maximize your positioning and everyone can see. Also, test to see if you need to dim the room lighting in order for people to see clearly. But avoid an extremely dark room, as it can be dangerous and also conducive to a sweet dream state. Get the machine in focus beforehand so your audience doesn't have to squint while you adjust on your first transparency.

It's best to turn the machine off when you are not using it. Don't expect your audience to sit and watch a blank screen. It's distracting and it hurts the eyes. Use a sticky note to cue yourself as to the exact time in your presentation when you will no longer need the projector.

Always have a back-up plan if you are depending on a mechanical device.

Always have a back-up plan anytime you have a dependent relationship with any mechanical device. They can rapidly make fools of us all. For instance, if your original lecture is dependent on using the overhead projector, be ready to also present it using a flip chart or chalkboard. Yes, Virginia, bulbs in overhead projectors do burn out, and they are hard to replace when you are in a resort with 20 executives who are impatiently looking at their watches. Some overhead projectors have a back-up bulb stored inside them. Although the bulbs are very expensive, anywhere from $25 to $40, some presenters carry an extra one in their emergency kit. But not one bulb fits all projectors.

While I'm mentioning back-ups it's also wise to carry an extra extension cord with a three-way prong adapter any time you are dependent on using an electrical visual aid. Completely cover the cord on the floor with heavy-duty tape so that no one, especially that presenter (you) who is trying to look oh-so-professional, trips and falls flat on their face.

■ *Flip Chart*–A really flexible low-cost aid; best used in groups of 50 or fewer.

When you are ready to write, pretend you are back in first grade. Use big, chunky lettering. A mixture of upper and lower case is easier to read than all capitals. Try to make them two to three inches high. It really depends on the size of the room and how far away the folks will be sitting from you. If time allows, draw a couple of words in different sizes and walk to the back of the room to test the legibility. Usually keep it to no more than 12 words to a page. Focus on using words, short phrases and symbols rather than full sentences. Colors are dramatic, but avoid orange and yellow as they are hard to read from a distance. Limit the variety of colors to no more than three per page. Change colors to emphasize a particular point.

Some flip chart paper even has faint lines every inch, just like that paper our grade school teachers passed out. Use those lines to help format the letters and keep them large. Simple cartoons and symbols such as circles and triangles are a terrific way to keep the page attractive.

Now here's a super technique to use which will make your presentation smooth and make you look like a true pro. Before the presentation, take a pencil and lightly draw the words and artwork on each page. Then during your presentation, just trace your markings with your colored marker pen. The audience cannot see the lines and you are never at a loss for words. You can also pencil in little notes to yourself in the margin that will keep you on track and focused. They might remind you of the next point, a key question to ask or an example you wish to relate. Or maybe just a prompt to smile more or take a deep breath. Just be sure you can read it and they can't!

Beware of pens that smell obnoxious and leak through to the sheet underneath. Newer pens have wonderful odors such as grape and licorice. If you should get the pens that leak through, use two pages at a time. If you have a chance, staple or paper clip them together so they can be turned together. And vow to find good pens that don't waste so much paper.

How many flip chart pages are too many? Good question. It rather depends on how they are being used. If you or a scribe are recording the group's ideas, take as many as you need. But if you are using the flip chart to aid you in presenting new material, I'd recommend no more than five charts in an hour.

If your handwriting is hard to read or if you wish to add some simple artwork to spice up your page, you can create your flip charts in your office. You can then use the same charts over and over again. Thicker paper is best for this. I've even been known to carry my flip chart pages on a plane. My trick is to tear off the sheets I've designed and roll them into large mailing tubes. That makes them easy to carry and re-use. Artist's tape instead of masking tape is easier to re-use and it still looks okay affixed to the corners.

Give some thought as to where you will stand to write on the flip chart. Practice it a few times. Also consider where you want the chart located in front of the audience. Since I am right-handed, I like to position the chart on stage left. In that way the participants can still see it and I can easily move away from it back to center stage. Of course, with charts that are affixed to the wall you do not have that flexibility.

If you plan to tear off used sheets and display them around the room, it's nice to have your tape already torn and ready to scoop up and use. Check the chart first. You may be lucky to have one of the new ones where the paper is a lot like giant sticky notes. The back top of each page is sticky and easily adheres to walls, windows or whatever.

Remember, you are using visuals to* AID *your presentation, not make the presentation for you.

While using the flip chart, white- or chalkboard, avoid speaking with your back to the audience. It makes it really difficult to understand you. This takes some practice at first. Either speak first, then turn and write or draw; or create the aid first, then turn and read to the group.

It's best to move a flip chart aside when you're done using it. Be careful. Some are a bit wobbly to move. This will give you more room to move in front of the group and you won't end up running into the equipment. Also, the viewers will not find it as distracting.

- *Whiteboard/Chalkboard*–Both the chalkboard and whiteboard offer us spontaneous visual aids that are very easy to use. They also give the convenience of easily correcting mistakes and adding or eliminating material. And, hooray, they are not dependent on any power source or mechanical equipment!

But alas, every time I approach a chalkboard I am convinced my dry cleaner smiles with glee. Invariably my clothes and hands end up covered with chalk dust. Please do as I say, not as I do. Avoid backing up and leaning on a chalkboard, and use a chalk holder.

Floating chalk dust is also hard on the throat. Be sure you have plenty of lukewarm water to sip while you are presenting.

Follow an outline format and use the same principles we looked at for using flip charts: mainly, keep it big and chunky.

These boards are superb for drawing diagrams, doing calculations and other demonstrations of your points.

If you thought it was advantageous, you might pre-draw something before your presentation. But, unlike the flip chart, it might be too distracting because it would be difficult to keep it concealed until you need it.

Do remember that your creation is temporary. If it's a real gem, it may be lost. Therefore, it may be best used in a more permanent visual aid such as an overhead transparency. Also, please remember to erase it when you are done. Believe me, you will grow to appreciate it when others do that for you.

Carry extra chalk and whiteboard pens plus an eraser just in case your meeting room has been raided and is missing these essentials.

- *Slide Projector*–A durable, somewhat portable aid that can have a powerful impact on an audience.

Like overhead transparencies, be sure that every slide supports your message. It's tempting to get swept away and use too many slides, thereby overwhelming your audience. Again, keep it simple and focused on your main points. Slides take both time and money to create, so put some thought into each one's effectiveness. They must look professional. The guidance of a graphic artist or a photographer can be very helpful in the design stage.

Rehearsing your talk with the slides will be invaluable to you. You will become familiar with the order of the slides and how to make the transitions. You will also become more comfortable about where to stand during your presentation and how you will use the equipment.

Limit the amount of time you will use slides, in order to minimize eye strain and prevent your audience from falling asleep in the dimmed setting.

Be sure to allow plenty of time to practice with the equipment just before your presentation, if possible. And always have a back-up plan, in case of malfunction.

■ *LCD Panel*–Place this flat computer monitor on your overhead projector and it will display what's on your computer screen. There are also units out that combine all these features into one box.

Keep it simple and focused on your main points.

These can definitely wow an audience, but don't get carried away. Remember, the presenter is you, not the computer. You are not there to merely operate the machinery. Your audience wants high-touch as well as high-tech! Relating good stories that are also humorous will help keep your presentation lively.

Of course, you need to be super-familiar with your equipment and ready to function in any emergency.

■ *VCR with Monitor*–Using videos is an excellent way to show rather than tell your message.

Be sure that your tape will be compatible with the facility's VCR and monitor.

Short tapes (10 to 15 minutes) or parts of long tapes are best. Remember, you are using this to underscore your points, not to make them for you.

Viewing a video is a wonderful way to foster a lively discussion afterwards. Focus the group's attention by asking them beforehand to think about a question or comments on a particular item they will be seeing.

■ *Props*—Now, before you pooh-pooh this idea as not being dignified or professional, give me a chance. What I am suggesting is using such props as silly hats, big tools made out of foam, beach balls that look like the earth, large cut-out pictures, etc. Dramatic props can really aid in retention and, when used well, they are just plain fun. The most effective learning takes place when people, especially adults, are relaxed

Dramatic props can really aid in retention and, when used well, they are just plain fun!

and receptive. I think this is particularly true when you are discussing heavy-duty topics such as death and taxes. How about showing oversized dollar bills to emphasize how people's financial lives will improve after following your program. Or pass out lemon and encourage them to make lemonade.

I know for some of you this may be a big risk, but give it a try. You will find it well worth it in results. Plus you will be memorable! Think back on a favorite presentation you've seen. You probably remember it because you had a good time first, and then you learned something.

Of course, like any other visual aid, you do not want to get overwhelmed by it. Try it on a small scale first and see how it works. As you become more comfortable using them, your audience will sense this and share in the good time.

Your willingness to have fun and perhaps play the fool a bit will make you much more approachable. People will like you and want to do business with you.

Also, think about using a practical prop. For example, if you are demonstrating effective phone techniques, use an actual telephone to show how to do it right.

GENERAL POINTERS ON USING VISUAL AIDS

Speaking of pointers—the tangible, extendible ones this time —they are awesome for emphasizing your point on a screen. Nowadays there are even some really impressive laser pointers. My only caution is that you don't get carried away. Be sure to get rid of it when you are done using it. This goes for a piece of chalk or a marker pen as well. Otherwise, it will take on a life of its own—doing flips as it flies between your hands, tapping out show tunes on a nearby table and even scratching certain hard-to-reach body parts. In other words, a funnel for all your nervous energy and a enormous distraction to your audience. Put these objects down as soon as possible.

Verify that whichever visual aid you use truly assists you in getting your message across and doesn't distract or overwhelm your audience.

Develop a back-up presentation in case something happens to your visual aids.

Remember, if your audience cannot see it, don't show it.

One last thought: You are your best visual aid. Be sure to dress professionally and remember to smile.

11

HANDLING THE PRESENTATION DETAILS SMOOTHLY

Many of the suggestions in this section apply to those of you who plan to self-sponsor your own presentations and therefore have complete control over the room logistics. But even those who speak as an invited guest on someone else's turf will find useful tips that will help to enhance your speaking environment.

USE NAME TAGS OR NAME TENTS

Name tents are used more often for seminars than for speeches. They should be placed on the table in front of the participants and in easy view of everyone else. Although once in a while you'll meet someone who doesn't want to use a name tag, most people don't mind them. Remember, many people are there to network with others. You will make it easier for them to meet and remember new people. It's nice to use people's names, especially during a question-and-answer session. When you do, people don't feel they are just meaningless faces to you. Remember, people's names will be very helpful when you are doing your follow-up. People are always honored when you remember them.

CHECK YOUR ROOM SET-UP

Be sure the room is set up as you requested.

I'm probably preaching to the choir here, but try to be polite to everyone—even the set-up people who didn't follow your instructions. I know it can be very frustrating when someone doesn't do their job, but make the best of it and remain as calm as possible. You must do whatever it takes to give your best to your audience.

CONTROL THE SEATING

It is really important that your group, especially if it is small, does not end up scattered throughout a large room. The empty seats seem to produce some sort of energy leaks and the isolation inhibits connection. Ask people as they arrive to move up front, or promote this by putting handouts only on the front seats. This also makes it easier for latecomers to slide in the back without disturbing others.

SET YOUR STAGE

If appropriate, you may wish to place your notes on the podium beforehand. Be sure that there is water to sip nearby. Check one more time that your props and visual aids are positioned where you want them and ready to go.

USE SIGNS TO TELL THEM WHERE TO GO AND WHAT TO DO WHEN THEY GET THERE

Detailed signs throughout the building will help people find you and alleviate some of their anxieties. Signs on your registration table are also helpful. In addition, people also like to know where the phones and restrooms are located. You can either make signs for these or announce their locations just before a break.

TOO HOT OR TOO COLD: IT'S A NO-WIN SITUATION

Find out if you can regulate the room temperature or at least open windows—more and more a rare occurrence. But realize that people's sensitivity to temperature can vary widely and you will not please everyone. I've even seen an extra line added to professional seminar brochures suggesting that participants wear layers of clothing so they can regulate their own comfort. I feel it is better to keep the room a tad cool, say 68°, so you won't have anyone taking a nap, especially right after a heavy meal!

HANDLING LATECOMERS AND THOSE WHO LEAVE EARLY

Try your best not to wait for those who are late. The ones who made it on time will appreciate the fact that you did start on time. Do not interrupt your presentation for the late arrivals. While speaking you can point out any empty seats for them and make sure they have a handout. Or ask an assistant to do this for you.

It's best to give people who leave early the benefit of the doubt. Yes, it can be disruptive, but just presume that they would not be doing it unless they absolutely needed to. Don't assume they left because of you or what you are saying—unless, of course, half the audience stomps out! Then it's time to review the delivery and design techniques presented in previous chapters.

DISABLED IN THE AUDIENCE

Sometimes if I see a disabled person in the audience, and if it seems appropriate, before I begin I introduce myself. Then I ask, "Is there anything I can do to make my presentation work well for you?" In my experience, these folks are very assertive in getting what they need and they are way ahead of me in setting up their space to maximize their viewing and hearing. But I still like to ask; mainly it's for my own benefit. It reminds me to be sensitive to the special needs of the folks in my audiences. Many have thanked me for making a point of asking, and they mention that many people, not knowing what to do, simply ignore them. It would be a big mistake to miss meeting these folks. Perhaps they'll become some of your best clients.

USING PLANTS IN THE AUDIENCE

This doesn't mean live plants, such as philodendrons. In carnival days, hawkers purposely placed people in the audience to move the crowd to buy. These folks were called shills. You're probably not planning a carnival act, but it is still nice to have amiable faces in your audience. Sometimes you can ask them to give you friendly but subtle cues, such as reminding you to smile or slow down, or how many minutes you have left. But asking them to comment to their neighbors about what a wonderful speaker you are may be going a bit far.

If you are new to your field and/or new to speaking, you might ask a more experienced person to sit in your audience and observe you. Their advice may prove invaluable to you.

WILL YOU LET THEM TAPE YOU?

Decide beforehand what your policy is about being tape-recorded. Many presenters do not permit it because they plan to sell tapes in the future. Others have no problem with it. Often people who ask have some sort of disability and listening to a tape afterwards aids their comprehension.

USING A MIKE

One of the best ways to find out if a speaker is an amateur is to watch, and listen, to what they do with a microphone. If you hear the fateful words, "Can everyone hear me?" or "Testing, 1-2-3," you know you are in for a long session. Here are numerous ways to prevent that happening to your audience.

Some speakers are uncomfortable using a microphone and opt to do without. This is a real disservice to the audience unless it is very small—say, less than 25 people. If people have to strain to hear you, that negativity will spill over into their feelings about you and whether you really care about them. Also, using a microphone is a kind thing to do for your voice.

> ***Using a microphone is a kind thing to do for your voice.***

Here are the four main types you will encounter:

1. *The Fixed-Lectern Microphone* – These are attached to the podium or lectern by an adjustable goose neck. Position the microphone below your mouth, so your audience can see your face. This set-up does not allow for any body movement. Basically you must stay where you are planted—right behind the mike. Be careful not to make dramatic hand gestures and hit the mike, sending static out to one and all. Inexperienced speakers may prefer this set-up as they are less exposed behind the lectern and they don't need to be very dramatic.

2. *Microphone on a Stand* – If you choose to keep the mike in the stand, you can only position yourself right behind it. Many speakers choose to take it out of the stand. Best to do this while it is turned off. Then, when you've got it in your hand, turn the switch on the mike on. This will give you lots more mobility, at least the length of the cord. And, by the way, don't get tangled up or trip on that cord. Hold the dangling cord in your opposite hand at your side in order to guide it away from your feet. Practicing really pays off with this.

Two disadvantages of this set-up are that the microphone can get heavy after a while even if you regularly change hands. Also, you may face the dilemma of what to do with the mike while you are writing on a board or flip chart. The best solution is to turn it off, gently place it on a table, write, then pick it up and use it again—after you turned it back on, of course. Practice holding a mike with one hand and your notes in the other hand.

3. *Lavaliere/Clip-On Microphone* – This is a much smaller mike that is either attached to a cord which goes around your neck like a necklace or clipped on to your clothing. Like the microphone on the stand there is still a long umbilical cord between you and the power source. But the tremendous advantage is that your hands are now free to make dramatic gestures and to utilize visual aids.

4. *Wireless Mike* – The microphone is clipped somewhere on your chest and a small transmitter box hangs in the back on your belt or waistband. Sometimes the box even fits in a pocket. There is a thin cord that attaches the mike to the box and it must be tucked inside your clothing. Another small cord that serves as an antenna hangs down from the box. (Rather like an animal's tail. Cute, huh?) This is by far the most versatile microphone available, and also the most expensive.

You are now free to move anywhere in the facility. Just be sure to hit that off switch on the box before you visit the restroom! This also applies to when you are having private conversations either before or after your talk.

Every once in a while if you are walking around a stage you may encounter a "hot spot" where the transmission is full of static or you pick up the conversation of a truck driver outside who is using a CB. Just walk away from that spot and avoid it for the rest of your presentation. If you are lucky enough to have an AV technician in the room when this problem occurs, give them a meaningful look and they'll take the corrective measures necessary.

If you're going to be using a clip-on mike give some thought to your clothing. Jacket lapels are best for attaching that mike. And suit coats, jackets and blazers are good for hiding that bulky box. Also, be sure you have a waistband or belt for the wireless mike box. Yes, I have seen some women get really creative when they were wearing a dress without a defined waist!

Another consideration in using mikes is that before you initiate any group discussion of your topic or a question-and-answer period, consider how well the audience members will be heard. It's best if they have their own mike and an assistant runs it out to them. If you are using a large microphone, like the TV talk show hosts, you may be able to share yours. But don't try this with a clip-on mike. It's awkward at best. It's a nice courtesy to repeat the question to be sure everyone has heard it before you give your answer.

When using a microphone always stifle any tendency to use close-in gestures such as beating your chest. The sound will definitely jar your audience.

Rehearsing with a mike is valuable. This extra effort will make you look like the professional that you are, and help you make the best use of a microphone in getting your message across.

Rehearsing with a mike will make you look like the professional that you are.

Be sure to refer to the Checklists Section of the Appendix. They will be extremely helpful to you in making sure that you have covered all your bases before you begin your presentation.

12

IT'S SHOWTIME: MAKE A POWERFUL DELIVERY

Even the driest subject can come alive if you use the following delivery techniques that will also sell you and your services and products.

THE START-UP WILL SET THE TONE

If you do not have anyone to introduce you, be sure to introduce yourself and say why you are qualified to present this material. Show your passion for the subject and your enthusiasm about having an opportunity to share it with them. It's a nice gesture to assure them that they made a wise choice to come listen to you. And then don't disappoint them.

Because adults really crave structure and their time is precious to them, give your agenda either in your handout or up front on a board or flip chart. Many will appreciate it if you are very focused and tightly organized.

If you are leading a seminar, alleviate the crowd's anxieties by announcing when the breaks will be, and the location of the phones, restrooms and vending machines. Tell the smokers where they can go. All of these details will send your group the message that you care enough about their comfort and satisfaction to find out this information for them.

If you have a small audience—usually under 12 people—you may want them to introduce themselves and state what they have come to find out. Asking what they expect is a practical way for you to adjust your material to meet their needs. For instance, one time I was giving a small business workshop and almost everyone mentioned a need to learn more about taxes and licensing. It was clear I needed to spend more time on that section and use a lot of examples. My flexibility was rewarded with very positive evaluations that even stated that it seemed the teacher knew exactly what they wanted to learn. They must have forgotten that they had already told me in the first five minutes of the workshop!

If the seminar is too large for individual introductions, have people pair up and introduce themselves to each other. Ask them to tell the other person why they came to this class. Then have the entire group report what they discovered. This is a nice way to encourage participation from the very beginning. Remember, many people attend seminars to fulfill their own networking goals. Introductions are an effective way to meet those expectations.

POINT OUT THE ROAD SIGNS ALONG THE WAY

Adults like to know where they are going. Do them a favor by occasionally summarizing your material and pointing out where you are on the agenda. This will give them a clear road sign as to where you are heading next. Just making a comment like, "Let's move on to point number three," can get everybody back on track, and perhaps assure your audience that you will get everything covered in time.

REPEAT YOUR KEY POINTS OFTEN

When I taught college accounting I believed that it would be insulting to adults to repeat a concept over and over again. I learned quickly. Many marketing experts state that we must be approached *seven* times before we make a buying decision.

As an information provider, plan to present your key concepts in a variety of ways so that your message gets across and is remembered. Did I mention that it's imperative to state your key points several times? Did you know that repetition really aids retention? (I think you got the point.)

THE POWER OF THE PAUSE

Taking a pause once in a while will do a favor both for yourself and your listeners. Some of us tend to speed up when we are nervous, have a lot of material to deliver or feel we are running out of time. But it is essential that we slow down and pause. First of all, using pauses gives us some breathing space and settles our nerves. If you think you won't get all your material delivered in the time slot, then it's time to slice and dice, not speed up.

Pauses also give your listeners a moment to rest and process the information. It will make listening to you much easier.

Plan your pauses by marking them on your notes. Try them often and you will see how effective they are.

Because many of us are uncomfortable with pauses, when they do come we cram them with some amazing things that we may not hear until we listen to a tape afterwards. But, believe me, your audience will hear all those fillers like "um", "ah", "you know", "okay?" Practice and experience will help you eliminate them, and that will really add to your credibility.

SELF-DISCLOSURE IS ESSENTIAL

One of the best ways to bond with the audience is through self-disclosure. Remember, many put you on a pedestal as the all-knowing expert. Revealing a funny story about yourself or relating your own life experience makes you real and approachable. Your ability to laugh at yourself will break down many barriers. Use these techniques every time you present.

SHOW, DON'T TELL

Although many of us were educated by the lecture method, it is imperative that we use other methods to get our message across. You probably didn't like it in school and neither will your listeners. If you have younger people in your audience, you will need to keep changing the pace because that is what they are accustomed to. It will dramatically reduce your quota of "yawns per minute." Thanks to TV, today's audiences are very visually oriented. Here's where visual aids can really enhance your presentation. Use the aids to illustrate case studies, demonstrations and examples.

Another way to show people what you mean is to brag about the successes of your clients (respecting their confidentiality, of course). You're proud of what your clients accomplish. Why not share it with others? A side effect of doing this is the message that it was you who contributed to your client's success. And if you can do it for those folks, you can do it for them.

TELL VIVID STORIES, ANECDOTES, ANALOGIES

There is a reason that great religious leaders use parables. They work. They create mental pictures that last a lot longer than mere words. Aim to share one of these for each of your main points. Review the comments in Chapters 3 through 5 on how to weave these into the design of your presentation.

ENTERTAIN AS WELL AS INFORM

Your audience will not be provided with their own personal remote control switch so that they can change channels whenever they are bored. Thank goodness. But it is important that you keep them interested as well as informed. Besides visual props and additions to your content that we have covered previously, consider adding humor to your presentation. Find a style which is comfortable for you. Using humor is a terrific way to keep your audience interested. Try a bit of drama, especially when you are telling stories, jokes or relaying examples. Shout. Gesture. Grimace. Move around the room. At first it may seem awkward, but with practice you'll become more comfortable and you'll find your audience will stay tuned.

WHEN TO ANSWER THOSE QUESTIONS

Decide how you wish to handle questions and announce your decision early on. If you do choose to handle any questions as they come up, instead of at the end, be sure you answer them fully. At the same time, it is important that you do not become sidetracked or let one person dominate the presentation. Some people will ask questions that relate only to their own situation. If you suggest that this person talk to you during the break or afterwards, the rest of the group will appreciate it.

Choose your questioners from different sides of the room.

When a person is asking a question, give them your full, undivided attention.

If you do not understand or are drawing a blank, ask the questioner to repeat it.

Always repeat or paraphrase the question, unless you are speaking to a very small group. There are a number of reasons for doing this. One, it gets people on the same wavelength. Those who did not hear the question the first time will be grateful for this courtesy on your part. Two, it gives you some breathing space to formulate your answer. And, finally, it helps if the session is being recorded so that the question is captured on the tape.

Make your answer very succinct and to the point.

Watch the questioner's body language. If you feel your answer did not satisfy them, ask them if you need to make it clearer.

When someone asks you a question, ask yourself why they are asking. (I'll bet you can't repeat that last sentence ten times over without stumbling!) There are variety of motivations for speaking up.

- Perhaps the person just needs attention and reassurance. If so, give it and move on.
- If they should challenge your opinion, try not to get defensive, but rather acknowledge that this is another point of view and move on.
- Of course, a listener could be genuinely confused. If that is the case and you suspect others are in the same boat, restate your point in different words and come up with another example. Another effective approach is to ask if there is anyone in the audience who can help illustrate the point in another way.
- If someone asks something and you don't know the answer, say you don't know. Don't apologize. Yes, even experts don't know everything! This response will build your credibility with your audience. Don't let your pride get in your way and try to fake an answer. Ask for that person's business card and promise to find out and get back to them. This will show how professional you are, and how committed to offering them quality service.

If you choose to hold the question-and-answer period at the end of your presentation, allow enough time for it and plan to wind it up with some closing remarks. For a 30-minute speech, plan on five to eight minutes for this section and firmly bring it to a close when time runs out. A cheerful story or a final call to action is a nice way to conclude.

END ON TIME

Maybe this is just a pet peeve of mine, but I feel it is essential that you end on time. Maybe even a tad early. It will show what a professional you are. It will also demonstrate that you respect other people's feelings and time commitments.

This is especially important when there are other speakers on the agenda. It's a lot like a doctor's office: once they get behind they never catch up. Maybe that's why I always try to get an early morning appointment!

First, make sure you have a clock or watch you can see. You may wish to pack a small travel clock that you can put on the podium.

Mark your notes as to what time it should be at various points. When you get to that point, you'll know whether you need to speed it up or stretch it out.

Designate parts of your presentation as "fudge paragraphs." Those are the stories, examples or even visual aids that can be dropped under a time crunch because the message is still complete without them.

Inexperienced speakers are often amazed at how much longer the actual time consumed was compared to their rehearsal time. Laughter, applause, questions from the audience and group exercises really gobble up the time. It's important that you allow for these.

13

WHAT YOU CAN DO TO BE A DYNAMITE PRESENTER

Even more than the words you present—you are the message. Here are proven techniques that will enhance your presentation.

THE PODIUM: NEITHER A BARRIER NOR LEANING POST BE

It's so tempting to hide behind and even hold on to the podium for dear life, especially if you are a beginner. Try to avoid it. It is better to move around because you appear to be more approachable to your audience. If you have memorized your stories and examples you're free to move into the audience and tell them. Just don't follow the example of some of my college professors and start pacing back and forth like a caged tiger! It's very annoying.

As you become more comfortable you will find ways to rest other than draping yourself all over the podium. When you assign group exercises or divide them into small discussion groups, take a mini-break yourself—sit down, use the restroom, get a breath of fresh air and a drink of water.

USE GESTURES

Use your body to emphasize your message. You might show how important your point is by hitting your fist into your open palm. Or move both your hands in unison to show similarities. You can walk closer to the group to relate a story or share a secret. Gestures of this type will make your presentation much more interesting. At first, gestures may seem very unnatural for you, but keep practicing. Watching your practice run on video will convince you to become more than just a "talking head."

LOOK 'EM IN THE EYE

Maintaining good eye contact is a way to establish credibility with your audience. Your participants will feel you are confident and have nothing to hide. Aim to speak to each person individually, rather than the group. Some presenters find it less nerve-racking to look at people's foreheads instead. As you look at a person, linger just a second or two and then move on to another. You'll soon find the friendly faces in the group and automatically gravitate to them.

YOUR VOICE WILL LOVE SOME WATER

Take tender care of your voice by taking sips of room-temperature water throughout your presentation. Pack your own water bottle just to be sure. Throat lozenges can also help.

THE SHOW MUST GO ON

Yes, you must go on even when you feel rotten or you are just not in the mood. Do whatever it takes not to disappoint your audience. They do not want to hear how awful you feel or what you had to deal with in order to get there—unless it's a funny story that helps you connect with them. Just get on with the show. Plus, you will find that once you get going you will feel better.

DRESS FOR SUCCESS

In today's world, "business casual" is very trendy. It is nice to be comfortable, but it is still important to dress very professionally when you are presenting. Make it a rule to dress a notch above what you think the best-dressed person in your audience will be wearing. Dressing in traditional business attire will greatly contribute to your credibility and to establishing yourself as an authority. It is possible to still be comfortable. And it's imperative that your shoes are. Also, be sure you have lots of pockets to hold marker pens and other items you may need while presenting. If you'll be using a portable microphone, a suit jacket or blazer works best.

OVERCOMING STAGE FRIGHT

The most powerful thing to remember is that your audience really wants you to succeed. That's what they're there for. Oh sure, occasionally you will get someone with really low self-esteem who feels they must tear you down in order to build themselves up, but this is rare. (Refer to Handling Challenging Participants further on in this chapter.)

Even the most experienced professional speakers still encounter nervousness. It is an indication that you really care about your performance and that you want to give your audience your best. As they say in Toastmasters: "You'll still have butterflies, but they are flying in formation!"

The single most important technique for reducing your nervousness is to be extremely well prepared. And that means you must practice, practice, practice. Use a tape recorder or, better yet, a VCR for your practice session. You will improve greatly after listening and seeing yourself. Each time you rehearse you will be giving yourself a confidence boost.

Be intimately familiar with your opening, conclusion and stories. They need to be presented smoothly so they have a strong impact. Usually it's the first three to four minutes of your presentation that are the most nerve-racking. A well-honed opening kicks you into automatic pilot where you stop focusing on yourself and spotlight your audience and your message instead.

> ***The most powerful thing to remember is that your audience really wants you to succeed. That's what they're there for.***

Bring along your notes and don't be embarrassed to use them if you must. Your audience would prefer that you get it right and stay on course rather than ramble on and on.

Never announce to your audience that you are nervous. Never make excuses to them. If you do, it will really sap your credibility. People will begin to question your message and doubt whether they should hire someone who lacks confidence. The old phrase, "Fake it 'til you make it," applies here. I know it seems your heart is pounding so loudly that everyone must hear it. But they don't. And I know that your knees may be shaking so hard it seems they won't support you. But they will. Your audience didn't come to hear about your trials and tribulations. They want solutions to their own problems. Don't ask them to focus on your nervousness instead of your message. Just keep going on the way you practiced and the audience won't be the wiser. Or, if they do detect nervousness, they'll empathize with you and focus on what you have to offer them instead.

Be sincere and passionate about your message. Become lost in it. The more you concentrate on your prospective clients and the important information—that they desperately need—the calmer you'll become.

Remember, you are changing people's lives. And the more you present, the more confident you will become.

Here's an excellent technique to really calm down beforehand. Circulate around the audience and introduce yourself. Shake their hands. Many of the participants are very flattered by this, particularly if you remember their names later. Ask them what they wish to get out of the talk. In other words, why did they come? This gives you a little bit of information as to how you can structure your material to meet their needs. When you begin your presentation, you won't feel as if you're talking to strangers.

Remember to breathe. I know it sounds funny, but taking deep breaths truly is calming, especially just before you start or when a participant is asking a challenging question.

Because you probably have a lot of adrenaline pumping in your system, it's a good idea not to add to the anxiety by being late or not knowing the exact location of the meeting room. Instead, get there early, check the set-up and get rid of some of that nervous energy by walking around the block or up and down a few flights of stairs. It works—just don't get sweaty!

Be aware of any negative self-talk before or even during your presentation. It can really sabotage you. Turn it around by using positive affirmation. Or focus on your goals and the important information your audience so desperately needs.

Sometimes our anxiety expresses itself in nervous gestures, such as fidgeting with clothes or small objects nearby. Once I saw a speaker completely shred a Styrofoam coffee cup before a presentation! Here are a few techniques that will keep nervous gestures under control:

- Take deep, calming breaths.
- Hold your hands in your lap while you are waiting to go on.
- Hold your arms at your side and resist the temptation to pick up any objects that you might start twirling, taping, flipping or whatever.
- Keep both feet planted solidly on the floor, even while sitting and waiting.

- Silently repeat to yourself encouraging affirmations such as, "I know I can do this."

If you feel that your stage fright is truly stopping you from achieving your goals, join Toastmasters (contact information is in the Appendix), take a speaking course or hire a presentation coach. This will give you further practice in delivery techniques. (Practice, practice, practice!)

Remember, the nervousness will not go away, but with experience you will learn to control it.

Here's a parting thought about nervousness. If you think you can do battle with it and conquer it, you will never win. It's lots more productive to think of nervousness as an energy source that will always be there and which you will learn to channel to your benefit. Use this force to be more enthusiastic and dramatic in getting your message across to your audience.

DANCE WITH YOUR AUDIENCE

As you become an accomplished speaker you will begin to read the signals the audience is giving you and adjust your presentation accordingly. In a way, it is a lot like dancing. Be aware of people's body language as you present. Are they slouching, yawning, doodling? That's a clear sign that you must change the pace, or maybe even suggest a break or group exercise. On the other hand, if they are perching on the edge of their chairs, giving you full eye contract, go ahead and expound on your point or elaborate on the story you are telling.

Don't assume that because someone seems to be scowling at you they are displeased. It often means that they are intensely listening and processing your information. Realize that in many audiences there will be a few folks you can't reach. Don't try to please everyone. Let them go and concentrate on the winners.

HANDLING CHALLENGING PARTICIPANTS

Drunks – If at all possible, try to avoid speaking to an audience that has been drinking. This is where some probing questions at the time of the booking really pay off. Drunks are rarely open to anyone's message and don't always respond to gentle joshing. If you are stuck with drunks, give it your absolute best shot. Consider trimming down your presentation to the basics. Eliminate the audio-visual aids—they'll be much too serious for this audience. Stay focused on your goal and remember there are probably some sober folks in the audience who are watching you. You will gain their undying admiration and, perhaps their business, if you keep your cool in this challenging situation.

Hecklers – It's important to try to determine a heckler's motivation. Take a deep, calming breath and trust your instincts in determining where this person is coming from. (Review my comments under the Q&A section in Chapter 12.) Believe it or not, these folks are creating a golden opportunity for you. Remember, the rest of the audience will be observing how you handle this. In this moment you have an opportunity to demonstrate qualities that can sell them. Your audience is deciding whether they should trust you with their business, so here's what you need to do:

1. Always treat the heckler with respect. Although it may get you a cheap laugh, calling them a derogatory name is never appropriate. Remember, it is vital that the heckler save face in front of others. If you humiliate them, others will join in their attack. If you can, call the heckler by their given name. It may establish connection and give them the recognition they crave.

2. Realize that what seems to you to be an attack may be a cultural thing. In some cultures testing an authority figure (that's you) is considered rude. In other

cultures, it is very acceptable behavior and a means of making you an insider—if you don't cave in, that is.

3. Of course, the biggest challenge for you is not to engage your emotions and get defensive. Nobody came to witness a fight. Your credibility is on the line here. You can stick by your opinions and not back down. And at the same time, simply acknowledge that some people feel differently without sharing your personal value judgment about it. Your goal is to get to the point where you and your heckler agree to disagree and then move on. Sometimes offering to speak with the heckler privately after the presentation can diffuse the matter.

4. Now be careful, but sometimes humor or a quotation works well here. Not as a way of attacking the heckler but as a way of relieving the tension and moving on.

Slow-Pokes – These are the folks who do not keep up with the rest of the group or whose questions are really off the mark. You will probably encounter these people more often when you give seminars than when you give short speeches. First of all, if you are coming across this situation frequently, you'll need to take a long hard look at yourself and the way you are presenting.

- Perhaps you could make your point more clearly with a better example or demonstration.
- Check to see if your agenda is clear so your audience can easily determine where you are taking them.
- When you assign a group exercise, be sure that your directions are clear. It works best to write them out as well as verbalize them. This will help some people who have different learning patterns.

It is important that you treat these folks with the utmost respect even though they can be rather frustrating. (Haven't we all been in this spot sometime in our lives?) At the same time, you cannot sacrifice the rest of the group while you try to bring one individual up to snuff. Ask their neighbor or the small group they are in to give them a hand. If you are lucky enough to have an assistant with you, see if they can work with them. Or, while the rest of the group is listening, explain your dilemma to the individual, ask if you can meet with them during the break or afterwards, and continue on with the program. Your sensitivity to the needs of others will establish trust and respect from those in your audience.

PREVENT DISASTERS

Your emergency kit (see the suggested content list in the Appendix) will help you deal with most physical problems. Knowing you're prepared will also calm you because you will be solving problems and keeping the show rolling.

BE PREPARED FOR EMERGENCIES

Remember that in case of an emergency, such as a power outage or fire alarm, you are the leader. You must be the calming voice in the storm. You may have a microphone and it will be your responsibility to lead people to safety. Be sure you know where the fire exits are and how to get help.

ENTHUSIASM IS YOUR TICKET TO SUCCESS

Despite the nervousness and the million details to remember, the one thing that will carry you to success is your own enthusiasm. Let it show. Be sure to let people know how much you care about what you are doing. (And if you don't care, get out of the business. You won't be able to hide it.)

One of the joys of making presentations is that it will renew your own excitement for your work and the important service you are providing.

Despite the nervousness and the million details to remember, the one thing that will carry you to success is your own enthusiasm.

Showing that you care will serve as a magnet for your audience. You will be perceived as very approachable.

You can show your audience that you care about their learning by offering a variety of training techniques, e.g., lecture, audio-visual, exercises, discussion, Q&A.

Be yourself. No one is fooled by phoniness for very long. Let your passion for your subject pour out.

14

TURNING YOUR AUDIENCE INTO CLIENTS AND REFERRALS

Now that you have given a great speech or seminar it's time to really get to work. This is the time to follow up with those who may become your clients. Using the suggestions in this chapter will help ensure your continued success.

DO THAT FOLLOW-UP

Now is the time to do whatever you planned and promised. Here are five things you can do to make another contact with those in your audience. Of course, this is presuming that you collected their names and contact information.

1. *Make phone calls.* The beauty of making these calls is that they are not cold calls. These people now know you and hopefully feel warmly toward you. Ask them how they liked your presentation. Inquire whether they had any questions or if there is something else you can make clear for them. Consider making some special offer to them, or ask how you can be of service to them.

2. *Send a letter, e-mail, or fax.* This would be personalized to them, and would explain your services.

3. *Give a questionnaire.* Offer some sort of incentive for completing it. The questions should point out the need for your services.

4. *Send a thank-you note.*

5. *Send anything you promised to send them.* This might be an article, more material or your newsletter.

PART OF THE PLAN

Do not assume that by giving speeches and seminars you will automatically get more clients and referrals. Instead, your presentations need to be just one part of your overall marketing plan. Sure, occasionally you will find some people who will hear you speak and want to start working with you immediately, but that is rare. You will get many more of your clients by doing other things to keep your name alive in their thoughts. In the Appendix you will find an excellent checklist to help you develop your marketing plan. I suggest you plan to do at least seven things in an 18-month period.

Here are some of the things I recommend:

- write an article for the organization's newsletter
- write an article for the local press
- write a report on your presentation for the organization's newsletter
- offer an "advanced" seminar
- send prospects a copy of an article or more information they may find useful
- send them a gift

Refer to the Appendix for a complete list.

READ THOSE FEEDBACK FORMS

Be gentle with yourself when you read your feedback forms. Remember, you don't have to be perfect—just genuine. There are going to be some people you will never please. Let go of them and concentrate on those who gave you positive feedback and helpful suggestions.

NOTE WHAT TO IMPROVE ON NEXT TIME

Soon after each and every presentation, find a quiet moment and jot down what seemed to work and what you plan to change next time.

If you recorded yourself, listen to the tape and make notes of the areas you want to improve on. Focus on the question-and-answer session and see if there are topics that you can make more clear next time.

CLEAN UP AFTERWARDS

Especially on college campuses, be sure to clean up your classroom afterwards. Take down any signs you posted in the building. You *never* want the continuing education department to get complaints about the mess you left. This is also true for hotels and conference centers. Of course, their crews are used to cleaning but you don't want to leave a big mess for them. You want the reputation that you are easy to work with.

THANKS FOR THE MEMORIES

It's a nice touch to write or call your program director the next day and thank them for all they did to make your presentation a success. Check out the example letter in the Appendix. It's a small gesture that will do wonders for your reputation.

It is also essential that you thank your referral sources for any leads they give you. They will want to know what happened. You may wish to check your profession's code of ethics regarding giving gifts to referral sources.

WHAT TO DO WHEN THEY ASK YOU BACK FOR ANOTHER GIG

It is very flattering to be asked to come back and present again. But before you say yes, ask yourself if it is worth it. Are you achieving your main goal? How can you make it even better—both for yourself and for your audience? Do you want to add an advanced class or a class on a related subject?

MARKET FOR MORE

If you would like to offer your talk elsewhere, the meeting planner can give you marketing ideas or a referral. See if this particular organization has a state or regional conference at which you could speak. Program planners often know each other and word-of-mouth is the best (and least expensive!) form of marketing.

MEASURE WHAT WORKS

For every presentation you make I have encouraged you to set goals. If you are using the copyright-free Intake Form which you can order at the back of this book, you will note that there is even a space for recording the results of your goals. As you give more and more presentations you will recognize the value of doing this. Studying your results will help you decide if you are reaching your target population and how effective you are at converting them to clients.

Recording results is going to be essential if you are self-sponsoring your own seminars and monitoring the costs. You will begin to see which promotional efforts are most effective. Did you ask on your feedback form how they heard about your seminar? Did you call all of your registrants the day before to remind them about the seminar?

Measuring what works will also help you to fine-tune your follow-up program. Did your prospects become clients after a phone call or because they read an article about you?

Studying your results will help you decide if you are reaching your target population and how effective you are at converting them to clients.

If you are not getting the results you want, it's time to take a long hard look at your presentation. Be sure to tape it or ask a trusted friend to observe and critique it. Are you being genuine and approachable? Is there anything you are doing or saying that may turn the audience off or make them distrust you? Are you appealing to their needs? Is it clear how working with you will make their lives better? Do they understand the value of getting your services immediately?

KEEP BUILDING YOUR CREDIBILITY

In this chapter, we discussed the importance of word-of-mouth advertising. I am convinced that your reputation is one of the most vital elements in continuing your success in any endeavor. You never want people saying that you do not deliver on your promises. Your word is your bond. If people trust you, they will give you their money because they know you will give them value in return. So this means you don't make promises unless you fully intend to keep them. Don't tell someone you will send them a flyer and then "forget." Don't say you'll call them in two weeks if you know you will not do it. These may seem like very small things, but I have seen countless small business owners fade away because they did not establish credibility with their customers.

15

BONUS: SPEAKING AS AN ADDITIONAL PROFIT CENTER

"How much do you charge?" That's usually the fateful question asked of us that opens our eyes to speaking as a lucrative profit center. "You mean people are paid for doing this?" Indeed they do, and plenty! But I feel I must warn you: you may find you enjoy professional speaking so much that you abandon your current profession!

FIVE STEPS TO GETTING PAID FOR YOUR PRESENTATIONS

1. EXPAND YOUR SPEECHES AND SEMINARS

It is important that you offer an entire menu of speaking options to those who might hire you. Your menu should consist of a variety of topics and lengths of presentations.

Each offering needs to be well thought out. Remember that professionals do not "wing it." They may *look* as if they are improvising, but they have spent hours practicing that effect. Professional speakers are paid well, but they also earn it.

Now is the time to take your original topics and expand them. One useful exercise is to look back on old feedback forms and see what other topics your audience wanted to hear. Review Chapter 2 on how to come up with popular topics. Just be sure that the subject is something you are passionate about and your audience will care about.

It is important to offer an entire menu of speaking options to those who might hire you.

If you've been presenting 20- to 30-minute speeches, you will need to expand them to 45 to 60 minutes, since that time slot is frequently requested for paid gigs. Take your original speech and see if you can add more examples and depth to each point. Or add one or two points. Perhaps you can add material from the things that people often ask in question-and-answer sessions. Develop some more audio-visuals that will help illustrate your points.

If you have been presenting seminars which last anywhere from one to two hours, it's time to punch them up to a half-day, full-day or even two or three days. Take each of your modules and bring in more material. Think of each module as a stand-alone one-hour seminar. Add more group exercises. Expand the handouts. Add more modules. Think about how you can use more examples that will demonstrate your points. Create a variety of visual aids. Don't forget to add more breaks and time for a meal.

2. DEVELOP A MARKETING PLAN THAT INCLUDES A BUDGET

Without the focus of a solid marketing plan it would be very easy to waste a great deal of money in marketing yourself as a speaker. Do your research and be sure that the market you are targeting really pays for speakers. Set realistic income goals for the next three years. Decide the best ways you will approach those who do the hiring.

Review all of the techniques in Chapter 7 for marketing yourself and your presentations. By implementing a variety of the suggestions made there, you will create a wellspring of demand for your presentations.

3. SET YOUR FEES

Your fees are really determined by your market. It's pretty typical to start out at $100 for a presentation. But this varies wildly depending on the group's budget and your negotiation skills. There is no set way to establish your fees, but do try to remain consistent so that one group does feel that you are not giving them as good a deal as you gave other groups.

Here's a good beginning range:

One-hour speech = $100 to $500 plus expenses
Half-day seminar = $350 to $750
Full-day seminar = $750 to $1,250

You might need to charge some combination of the above fees if they ask you to present, for example, a keynote speech and a breakout workshop.

Another consideration about fees is your travel expenses. If your speaking gig is across the state or across the country, you'll need to build your time and expenses into the fee.

Of course, if you are self-sponsoring your own seminars, your fees are determined by the net take. Research the market and find out what most successful folks are charging for their seminars. Develop a budget and keep your overhead costs to a minimum.

4. CREATE YOUR PROMOTIONAL MATERIAL

Meeting planners who work for associations or corporations are accustomed to seeing some pretty sophisticated marketing material from speakers. It is important that you think about the image you want to convey.

Now is the time to pull together a very professional-looking press kit. It should contain your photo, your "bio," a description of your presentations, any articles written by you and those testimonial letters you have collected along the way. Many professional speakers also include an audio or videotape of a presentation and their fee schedule. Refer to the discussion in Chapter 7 and the Examples Section of the Appendix.

5. PRODUCE PRODUCTS TO SELL

Another superb way to make money speaking is to sell products at the back of the room.

The logical place to start is with your handouts. Now is the time to copyright any material you plan to sell. Information on how to do this is in the Resource Section of the Appendix.

Here are two ways you can go with these.

1. Expand them into a good-sized workbook and charge the meeting planner extra for these to be supplied to each member of the audience.
2. Expand them so that they are valuable, stand-alone products that your participants will want to purchase after your presentation, and sell them at the back of the room. If you have done a great job presenting, people will be eager to take a part of you back to their office and these types of products are a terrific way to do this.

Now let's think about other spin-off products you can offer people at the back of the room. By the way, don't think you need to produce all of these. Many speakers start out by selling other people's products until they develop their own. Probably the next logical product to develop is a cassette tape of your presentations. Easy to do if you've been recording them. Now let's really get creative. Here we go:

article reprints	bookmarks
books	calendars
booklets	caps

- data sheets
- mugs
- posters
- quote books
- reminder cards
- software
- special reports (5 to 10 pages)
- T-shirts
- tip sheets
- videos
- worksheets

Once you start brainstorming the ideas just flow.

Here's another thought to consider as you develop speaking as a lucrative profit center. Think about donating 10% of all profits to your favorite charity. Besides knowing that you are doing a good thing, it will keep you motivated during the challenging times. Don't hesitate to mention this policy to your buying audience.

TEN GREAT WAYS TO MAKE MONEY SPEAKING

1. OFFER SELF-SPONSORED WORKSHOPS WITH HEFTY REGISTRATION FEES

If you have been offering self-sponsored seminars for a fairly low fee, or free, just to bring in clients, you may have gotten the feeling that you were sitting on top of a gold mine. You are absolutely right. We are living in the booming Information Age and people are desperate for information. They and their employers are willing to pay big bucks to get it. Despite that rosy picture, many have lost thousands trying to run seminars. Be sure you study your market well. You need to be certain you have a hot topic and that people are willing to spend money for your information. You also need to realize that you will need to devote a great deal of time and money in marketing your seminars. But if you do it right there is plenty of money to be made. Read the seminar books listed in the Resource Section of the Appendix.

2. GIVE KEYNOTE SPEECHES

Hundreds of keynote speeches are given every day. They start off conventions, conferences, retreats and many other types of meetings. Fees can range anywhere from $100 to $25,000 and up if you are a celebrity.

If you decide to offer keynotes, remember that they will need to be very motivating and uplifting. Plan to present them with high energy and in an enthusiastic manner.

Contact your local convention center and chamber of commerce to get a list of the meetings that are planned for the next few years. Contact these organizations and send them your fancy press kit. Follow up with a phone call to see if they are interested in hiring you.

3. HIRE OTHERS TO PRESENT YOUR MATERIAL

You know your material is good, but you don't want to take time away from your professional work to make paid presentations. Well, hire a dynamite speaker to present your material. This person should be an accomplished speaker since they are really representing you. You can set them up as an employee, a contractor or a franchisee. Just be sure you have a contract and a clear understanding of how this arrangement will work.

4. SELL YOUR LESSON PLAN PACKAGE TO OTHERS IN YOUR PROFESSION

Why not save others in your profession from re-inventing the wheel? You've already done all the prep work, pulling together a program that works well to attract new clients. Consider sharing it—for a fee—with others.

It probably won't take much to turn your presentation notes into a guidebook for others to use. Your audio-visual aids and handouts can also be included in the package.

5. OFFER YOUR EXPANDED PROGRAMS AT THE CORPORATE, NATIONAL AND INTERNATIONAL LEVEL

It's time to refer to the *Encyclopedia of Associations* mentioned in Chapter 1. Not only does it give you a great many details about tons of associations, but it also lists when and where their next big convention will be. If you have presented to a group at the local level, ask them for a recommendation. Find out who the meeting planner is and send your press kit. Study the organization's publications so you know which of your topics would best fit their audience. You might even consider renting a trade booth and selling your services and your products at their show.

Start a list of corporations who may hire you. Network with people who work for these organizations and ask them about their training programs. Many companies bring speakers in for a "brown bag" lunch meeting with their employees. This is an outstanding way to get exposure and open the door to longer, more comprehensive presentations. Contact the training department, human resources department or sales division to see if they hire trainers. Pitch your presentation over the phone or send them a letter and your press kit.

As you become more and more in demand and your speaking fees increase you may consider working with a speakers' bureau. Many charge as much as a 25% commission on your fees, but they will do a lot to promote you and book some great speaking engagements for you.

6. SPONSOR YOUR OWN CONFERENCE OR SYMPOSIUM

Why not string all of your topics together and offer an all-day event? One super way to do this is to offer an advanced seminar to those who have already participated in one of your presentations. If you have given them value, they'll be delighted to have more time with you.

Or ask your colleagues to present, too. Find other professionals who offer a complementary service and present an all-day symposium to the same target market. You may have seen these types of events pitched to those about to retire. Usually it's a team of professionals – lawyers, CPAs, insurance agents, CFPs, etc., who make the presentations. And reap the profits both in dollars and in clients.

7. ENTER INTO A JOINT VENTURE WITH OTHER BUSINESSES

Partnering with others is an excellent way to share the costs as well as the profit. Another professional may not want to do the speaking and will gladly hire you to represent them and send them clients.

Think creatively about who might sponsor you. It's possible that a software company or an office supply store would be happy to underwrite your presentation.

8. OFFER CONTINUING PROFESSIONAL EDUCATION CLASSES

It probably would not take much to have your current seminar approved by some state board for continuing professional education. Thousands of professionals need to take these classes yearly in order to maintain their licenses. Sponsoring organizations are always looking for a fresh approach and new topics. Don't just think of your own profession: usually it's other professionals who need to be kept updated on the latest in your field. For instance, a CPA may present the latest tax law to a group of lawyers. Or a psychologist may update health care providers about the latest treatment approaches. Not only can you make money from offering these classes, but you may get some great referrals because you have established yourself as an expert in your field.

Plan to present the participants with a certificate of attendance at the end of the class. Not only is it a nice touch to recognize a day of hard work and fun, but many will need it to verify the completion of the class so they can receive credit.

9. CONSULT WITH OTHERS WHO WISH TO MAKE PRESENTATIONS

Now that yo've made several presentations, you have gained a great deal of wisdom on how to make presentations. Consult with the neophytes who are just thinking about making some presentations. Most will be very willing to pay in order to shorten their learning time and ensure their own success.

Besides the money, you may find that you receive two additional benefits from offering these services. First, you may experience great joy in helping another become successful. And second, it will improve your own presentations. Not bad, huh?

10. SELL PRODUCTS

Selling your own spin-off products or products of others can become very lucrative for you. Most people start by offering their audiences certain products for sale at the back of the room. If you have done a good job presenting, people will be eager to cement their learning with more information.

Go back to Chapter 8 and review the techniques for promoting your services from the platform. You will need to do the same things in order to promote your products. But do be very careful here, as most audience members resent it if a great deal of time is spent on a rambling sales pitch.

You will also need to plan out exactly how you will stage the selling. Will you need to run to the back of the room after your speech to do the selling yourself? Or will you have an assistant? Think about how you can set up an inviting display of your products that will attract your audience. Plan to pack a cash box so you can easily make change. Be sure to check out the sales tax laws in the state where you are presenting. Consider getting a merchant status so that you can process your customers' credit cards.

Be prepared to autograph any written material you are selling. People like to have what they buy be personalized by you.

Another way to sell your products is through your newsletter. Write up a enticing description of the product and how it would be benefit for your readers. Include an order form or ask them to phone in their orders. Make it as easy as possible for them to buy from you.

Still another way to sell your products is to offer a special promotion to your clients and others on your database. Send them a special mailing that may include a reduced price or a bonus product. These strategies will give them the extra incentive to order immediately.

If you have created a useful product that is selling well, you might consider renting a mailing list and selling it through direct mail. Resources are listed in the Appendix.

Still another idea is to create a catalog of all your products. Send it out to those on your database and to any mailing lists that you rent.

Remember to market your products by sending out publicity releases to the media each time you create a new product.

CONCLUSION

Often I caution professionals not to data-dump on their audiences, and yet I know I have given you a lot of data in this book. Hopefully you have been savoring it in bite-sized morsels and contemplating how you can apply this information in your business life.

Giving speeches and seminars is one of the best, low-cost marketing tools you can use. You now know all the steps to take. You also have very specific suggestions on how to not let your fear of public speaking immobilize you.

The next step is yours. You can either put this book on your reference shelf, never refer to it again and wonder why you don't get more clients and referrals; or you can start following the guidelines in this book and keep referring to it again and again. Will it be effortless? No. But it will be well worth it. And maybe even fun.

If you have never given presentations before, start by taking small steps and build on your successes. Like many other skills in life, you get better only by doing it over and over again. Realize that you will not be perfect, and that is perfectly okay. Your prospects deserve to hear your message.

APPENDIX: EXAMPLES

TELEPHONE SCRIPT TO BOOK SPEAKING GIGS

Good morning. May I please speak to the person in charge of *(training or scheduling speakers)?*

Hello. This is ____________________*(your name).* I'm an __________ *(your title)* and I am interested in making a presentation to your group. I speak on ______________ *(topic).* Is that something your group might be interested in?

Great.

At this point they may want more information on your topic. Give them your one-minute commercial which was discussed in Chapter 7.

They may then start talking about dates. Start filling out your intake form.

Or, if they seem a bit reluctant, offer to send your press kit by saying:

Well, what I'd like to do is send you a packet of information about my material and call you back in a week or so to talk more about how we could work together.

Thank you for your time. Have a great day.

OFFER-TO-SPEAK LETTER

Dear _______________ :

May I help you plan one of your group's programs? I would be pleased to make a presentation on one of my most requested topics:

- ____
- ____
- ____
- ____

These and other topics relating to my expertise in the field of ____________________ could be tailored for your group.

Each of the sessions is designed to give concrete guidelines and practical tips based on my __ years of business experience. I have presented these programs to business and community groups with good success.

Please call me at (___) __________ for more information.

Cordially,

◆ **CHECKLIST**

- Be sure the meeting planner's name is spelled correctly.
- Mention if you are a member of this group or have attended their functions.
- You may wish to elaborate on what qualifies you to speak on this topic.
- Tell why your topic would be of interest to this group.
- If appropriate, offer to share testimonial letters or references from other successful speaking gigs.

Options to be offered in this letter or at the time of booking your speaking gig:

- Offer to write an article for their publication. Can run just before you present. Might also offer to run a second article as follow-up to your presentation.
- Volunteer to write news releases and/or work with their publicity person.
- Offer your publicity photo for their use.

Plan to call them and follow up if you do not hear from them in a reasonable amount of time (two weeks?).

THANK-YOU LETTER

Dear ___________ :

Thanks very much for inviting me to speak to your group. I appreciate the opportunity and thoroughly enjoyed it. The group was very _______________. I felt I was making a real contribution.

Please let me know if there are other organizations that might enjoy hearing me speak.

All the best,

APPENDIX: CHECKLISTS

CHECKLIST FOR THE DAY BEFORE YOUR PRESENTATION

- ❑ breath mints
- ❑ business checkbook to write refunds
- ❑ chalk and/or whiteboard pens
- ❑ list of those pre-registered
- ❑ copies of all handouts & feedback forms
- ❑ copies of case study
- ❑ extra name tags
- ❑ facilities information including map and room number
- ❑ flip chart pages in round carrying case
- ❑ display items
- ❑ presentation notes binder with case study
- ❑ power food
- ❑ marker pens (7)
- ❑ money pouch with $ for making change
- ❑ my business cards
- ❑ name tags and pen
- ❑ props
- ❑ room signs
- ❑ tape
- ❑ transparencies
- ❑ water bottle

CHECKLIST FOR THE DAY OF YOUR PRESENTATION

- ❑ check out any equipment used during the presentation
- ❑ examine clothing, hair and face
- ❑ eat a energy-producing meal beforehand
- ❑ target parking spot and have $ to pay
- ❑ empty bladder
- ❑ chalk/pens ready to use
- ❑ extra name tags ready to distribute
- ❑ prepare all handouts
- ❑ set up display table
- ❑ know name & contact number of AV person to assist
- ❑ locate restrooms
- ❑ locate telephones
- ❑ my name displayed
- ❑ name tags on table with pen
- ❑ presentation notes ready
- ❑ room signs out
- ❑ sit in back of room and see what it feels like
- ❑ water bottle filled

These are checklists I use for one of the workshops I present at a local college. Feel free to adapt them to your own needs.

SPEAKER'S EMERGENCY KIT

- ❑ batteries
- ❑ binder clips
- ❑ breath mints
- ❑ change of shoes
- ❑ clear nail polish
- ❑ extension cord, long, with three-prong adapter
- ❑ extra name tags or name tents
- ❑ extra plain white paper
- ❑ first-aid kit
- ❑ flashlight
- ❑ glue stick
- ❑ grooming aids such as a small mirror, comb, etc.—plus for women, an extra pair of pantyhose, lipstick; for men, a replacement tie
- ❑ if using a chalkboard, chalk and eraser
- ❑ if using an overhead projector, extra pens, transparencies, an extension cord and even a replacement bulb (although they are very expensive and don't work in all machines)
- ❑ ink pens
- ❑ list of emergency phone numbers

- ❑ original of my handout, so extra copies can be made for the unanticipated crowds that appear eager to hear me talk
- ❑ paper clips
- ❑ pre-moistened towelettes
- ❑ rubber bands
- ❑ safety pins
- ❑ scissors
- ❑ small clock that can be placed on the podium
- ❑ small tool kit including hammer, screwdriver, knife and nails
- ❑ measuring tape or ruler
- ❑ sponge with plastic sandwich bag to take it home wet
- ❑ stapler with staples in it
- ❑ string or twine
- ❑ tape—masking and transparent, also duct
- ❑ thread and needle
- ❑ throat lozenges
- ❑ thumb tacks

FOLLOW-UP MARKETING PLAN

Presentation ______________________________

Date of presentation ______________________________

Check at least seven and plan to complete them within 18 months of giving your talk.

MARKETING ACTIVITY	GOAL DATE
❑ submit news releases to local media	________
❑ send sales letter to participants	________
❑ distribute a questionnaire to participants	________
❑ send follow-up material (article, booklet, etc.)	________
❑ offer "advanced" seminar	________
❑ invite to open house at your office	________
❑ make follow-up phone calls to participants	________
❑ send follow-up e-mail to participants	________
❑ mail thank-you notes	________
❑ send participants newsletter	________
❑ submit article to organization's publication	
❑ place advertising in organization's publication	________
❑ fax sales message to participants	________
❑ give gifts	________
❑ submit report on your presentation to organization's publication	________
❑ offer free half-hour consultation	________
❑ offer coupons	________
❑ ______________________________	
❑ ______________________________	
❑ ______________________________	

Notes

Notes